Date Due

F

THE REJECTION SYNDROME

Charles R. Solomon

Tyndale House
Publishers, Inc.
Wheaton, Illinois

Scripture quotations are from
the King James Version of the Bible.

First printing, October 1982
Library of Congress Catalog Card Number 82-50698
ISBN 0-8423-5417-4
Copyright © 1982 by Charles R. Solomon
Printed in the United States of America

CONTENTS

ONE
Setting the Stage
17

TWO
The Syndrome in Operation
29

THREE
Crises and the Cross
53

FOUR
*Rejection—Results of
the Fall*
73

FIVE
Accepted in the Beloved
80

SIX
The Effect of Rejection on Identity
85

SEVEN
*Living to Succeed—
Identity through Doing*
91

EIGHT
*Succeeding to Live—
Identity through Dying*
96

NINE
Man: Dichotomy or Trichotomy
99

TEN
The Church, the College, and Counseling
111

ELEVEN
The Church, Rejection, and Humanism
122

TWELVE
God's Answer to a Rejecting Society
137

FOREWORD

God has set eternity in our hearts, which drives all of us to seek true fulfillment, meaning, and purpose in life. As Christians, we intellectually acknowledge that this fulfillment is not earthbound. Our deepest longings are not temporal but eternal, because we are spiritual creatures.

If we believe these truths, why are the lives of most Christians characterized by spiritual mediocrity? Why is there so much compromise, defeat, and conformity to the ambient value system of our culture? There are a variety of reasons, but the root problem is that the majority of believers are tapping the wrong source of life. They find their identity in temporal relationships and possessions and define themselves in terms of people, places, things, and experiences. The Preacher of Ecclesiastes thoroughly explored all of this territory and concluded that none of these things can satisfy us for long. There has to be something more.

A person can profess Christ but continue to live his own life, which leads only to frustration and emptiness. All believers acknowledge the death, burial, resurrection, and ascension of Jesus Christ, but few have entered into an understanding of their co-crucifixion, burial, resurrection, and ascension with Christ. Only when we see Christ as our life and walk in the power of his Spirit will we experience real fulfillment and victory over the power of sin.

Dr. Solomon shows in this book that the concepts of acceptance and identity are inextricably bound together. The many forms of overt and covert rejection that we experience in our relationships with others can devastate our self-image unless we see ourselves as unconditionally loved by God and "accepted in the beloved" (Ephesians 1:6). God's gracious acceptance of us in Christ is unaffected by our circumstances or performance. Thus, our real identity is not based on what we do but on who we are.

The Holy Spirit has been bringing a rapidly growing number of Christians into an understanding of Christ not only as their Savior and Lord but also as their life. In recent years, God has used books like Charles Solomon's *Handbook to Happiness* and David Needham's *Birthright* to spread these truths. Some of the terminology in *Birthright* is different, but a closer analysis will reveal that both men have come to the same conclusions.

Because their view of the spiritual life is so different from the standard (and largely ineffective) teaching on this subject, several misunderstandings have surfaced. Such misconceptions are inevitable, because it is difficult for us to consider openly and fairly an alternate model while clinging tenaciously to the one we were taught. The perspectives we have embraced become quite comfortable like a pair of old slippers, and there is a natural tendency in us that resists change.

Red flags like "passivity" and "perfectionism" are often raised as a convenient way of dismissing any teaching about the exchanged life. It is easy to hurl labels, but in this case, the labels just don't stick.

1. *The exchanged life (Christ's life for our life) does not mean passivity.* It involves a series of active choices to walk in conformity with who we are in Christ. We must decide to walk in dependence on the power of the Spirit and not after the flesh.

2. *This teaching does not mean perfectionism.* Writers like Solomon and Needham repeatedly say that an understanding of our identification with Christ does not produce immunity from sin.

3. *The spiritual apprehension of our co-crucifixion and co-resurrection with Christ should not be equated with the idea of a "second blessing."* Our understanding of the truths in Romans 6—8 does not make them happen to us. They were ours when we became new creatures (2 Corinthians 5:17) in Christ.

4. *Our participation in Christ's death and resurrection does not mean that we contributed to the atonement of our sins.* This was entirely the work of Christ on our behalf, and we are the recipients of this undeserved gift.

The abundant life and the abiding life are one and the same. We give up nothing when we turn away from the self-life to the Christ-life. "If any man will come after me, let him deny himself, and take up his cross, and follow me. For whosoever will save his life shall lose it: and whosoever will lose his life for my sake shall find it" (Matthew 16:24, 25).

Kenneth Boa
Director of Research and Development, Search Ministries

INTRODUCTION

The role of rejection as a destructive force to the personality has been overlooked or given only fleeting attention by many who work in the behavioral sciences. When they do discuss rejection, the weight of emphasis is given to the blatant, obvious destruction of a person or persons by others.

Though rejection may well include dislike or even hatred of someone, such is not always the case. Rejection also takes place when a person receives massive doses of "smother love" or when acceptance is contingent upon satisfactory performance.

Rejection occurs when love is withdrawn, knowingly or unknowingly, and when a person is denied the right or opportunity to be or become a person. Rejection might be defined as the absence of meaningful love at the best and of wanton disregard of another person and his needs at the worst.

People don't usually bring up the subject of rejection until their lives are at the desperation point. Persons who give more rejection than they receive may become very defensive and vocal in denying that they are doing so to avoid facing the inevitable guilt feelings that come from their negative influence on the lives of others.

On the other hand, recipients of such rejection may welcome an explanation of what has been responsible for their psychological symptoms and lack of effectiveness in living. Such understanding does not justify continued irresponsible living. Nor does the understanding of the cause merely shift the blame for bad behavior from those who are being rejected onto those who are rejecting them. It does provide a basis for self-understanding, which becomes foundational to receiving and appropriating the answer.

It is obvious that such a universal syndrome would permeate all levels of society and its institutions. Since no one but God is capable of giving perfect love at all times and in every circumstance, some lack of love or imperfect love (rejection) will come into all of our lives. Rejection occurring early in childhood and the severity of that rejection are usually determining factors in the amount of damage sustained by the rejected personality.

Those who have been rejected are prone to pass along some form of rejection to those closest to them. Until those who have been rejected find the life-transforming love of Christ as the only complete antidote to rejection-based symptoms, they turn to pursuits which they hope, consciously or unconsciously, will make them acceptable to themselves and others.

In these pursuits of acceptance, the hidden agenda is frequently more important than the one open to public view. Being president of a company brings its rewards financially, but the prestige and acceptance it buys may well outweigh monetary considerations. Being zealous in service for the Lord, whether as pastor or lay person, may well be done more to achieve the adulation of others than as a result of God's leading. Such service becomes an end in itself.

Perhaps it is not too great a generalization to state

that many, if not most, major accomplishments in the world are, at least in part, motivated by a desire for self-aggrandizement. Many people are hurt, if not destroyed, in the wake of such selfish pursuits of glory.

Such a person, not having found meaning in an *identity* based on mutual love, sets about to build an identity based on performance. The concepts of acceptance and identity are so intertwined it is impossible to discuss one without the other. Either a person is accepted for who he is or any acceptance received will be based on his appearance, his performance, or his possessions.

Prestige, power, and possessions become the medium of exchange to satisfy the consuming passion for acceptance—the hidden agenda which may be unrecognized by everyone involved, including the person himself.

The humanistic thinking inherent in this process has so permeated society—even the church, where one's identity should be found in Christ rather than in performance—that it is tantamount to sacrilege to call a person's motivation into question.

Either a person will find acceptance and identity in Christ as free gifts, or he will find it necessary to set about to earn both; the former is grace while the latter is works. To put it another way, the former is of the Spirit and the latter is of the law (self-effort)—a manner of life fraught with humanistic thinking.

Humanism is a word that has been used many different ways. During the so-called renaissance period the word was understood as the revival of classical studies, an emphasis on secular concerns. The philosophy which goes by that name today is often defined in all-or-nothing terms, to the point that true Christianity and humanism are mutually contradictory. Many people today understand humanism to be a man-centered philosophy which has no place for God. This form of humanism, or so-called secular humanism, has so infiltrated our way of thinking that much that purports to be Christian is really work done for God in man's strength or human effort.

Some of the most ardent believers of the past spent many of their early years working for God in dedicated self-effort only to find that they must be broken of self-dependency through adverse circumstances. Though surrendered to the Lord and desirous of being totally obedient, they found they had been doing many of the right things, but not recognizing the difference between working in God's strength and trying to do God's work in their own strength. These same believers would have given mental assent to the closing phrase of John 15:5: ". . . for without me ye can do nothing." Yet their efforts denied this truth that Jesus taught.

Many of these servants of the past later testified to a breaking process through which they passed, culminating in the experience of co-death and co-resurrection with Christ. The experienced Cross of Galatians 2:20, the appropriated death and resurrection which the Scriptures say was ours through identification, became a reality for them. Although this death and resurrection took place when Christ experienced it, its effect on us becomes a reality when we understand and accept it as a fact.

When the word *humanism* is used, it is not intended to label such believers as charlatans or heretics but to point out that humanism is *self-dependency* or trusting the arm of the flesh. Such efforts may be blessed of God, but they lack the full empowerment available to those who believe. Much of the credit can rightfully go to man for ministry or work done in his own strength even though God has clearly stated, ". . . I will not give my glory unto another" (Isaiah 48:11).

A modified form of humanism exists where the centrality of the Cross is omitted in things spiritual, not to mention in the secular realm. We need to investigate the emphasis being placed on self-effort or do-it-yourself Christianity as it relates to the individual, the church, educational institutions, and society at large. One has only to peruse the shelves in bookstores, Christian and secular, to see the emphasis placed on self-help. Many Christian books on psychology in its varied forms and applications are strangely silent about the need for experiencing the Cross in dealing with human behavior problems. Christians do not always discern the subtle influence of humanism inherent in psychology and other "how-to" books about the Christian life in which the meaning of the Cross is obscured or is not central.

It is incumbent upon us who try to teach others of the love and life of the Lord Jesus Christ to teach and preach a pure gospel. Rampant humanism affects and infects our thinking until much that we say and do may not be of faith, though our motivation may be to serve our Lord with all our being.

I have sought to address the issues of rejection, and the rejection syndrome, as I have labeled it, in a spirit of love. The need to be clear in our thinking about the humanistic bias of self-effort must be understood. All that is of the flesh must be submitted to the Cross for purification. It is time for judgment to begin at the house of God.

Only as we realize in experience our acceptance in the Beloved and find our identity—our life—in him will we be free of enslavement to selfish motivation, emotional programing, based on past rejection, and a lifestyle heavily influenced by humanistic thinking.

A more definitive coverage of the topic of rejection may be found in the author's first book on the subject, *The Ins and Out of Rejection*, which is available through Cross-Life Expressions, 1455 Ammons Street, Denver, Colorado 80215.

SETTING
THE STAGE
One

A few years ago I received a letter from a representative of the Sudan Interior Mission, which ministers on the continent of Africa. He told of a young lady we shall call Olga whom he had met in the heart of Africa. She had experienced great difficulty in her home in Germany and decided to join a mission group (not the SIM) and go to Africa to "find herself." Upon doing so, she "found herself" in the country of Niger, and just as miserable as she had been in Germany.

While there in Africa she happened upon a copy of *The Ins and Out of Rejection* and found not only the understanding of her symptoms but also the cause of the problem and its solution. Though she was involved in a ministry to others, she had never come to know the Lord Jesus Christ in a personal way. Changing geography did not change her person. Her father was a physician, her mother an artist, and her brother was a communist professor in a German university. Through reading the book she gained an understanding of the rejective patterns she had experienced, the absence of meaningful love in her family situation.

The Spirit of God brought the message of the book

home to her as she read it, and she found in the Lord Jesus Christ deliverance from her sins and her self-centeredness. Shortly thereafter, she returned to Germany and was instrumental in seeing her parents and her brother come to Christ.

Rejection had driven her to an intercontinental search for meaning which is to be found only in a Person—never in places, things, or altruistic pursuits. Once she found salvation in Christ and understood her identity in him, she prepared herself for the mission field by receiving Bible training. She returned to Africa under another mission organization and I understand she is there now, being used of God.

THE UNIVERSAL QUEST

Millions of persons around the world are searching for meaning in what to them is becoming a more and more meaningless world. Most of them do not have a personal relationship with the Lord Jesus Christ. Many Christians are also still caught up in the mad race to find meaning and acceptance in the pursuit of things and relationships. Although people, power, prestige, and possessions may provide fulfillment for a period of time, none of them has eternal significance. For these people there remains a void which is never quite satisfied, and the quest continues throughout life with only the object—not the objective—changing at different stages of life.

The unrelenting quest for acceptance takes many forms. The doggedness of the quest proves that such people are driven by a compelling need. With rare exceptions, people do not expend all of their resources to reach a goal unless they are goaded by some extreme need. My experience in counseling has shown that most people going through such meaningless struggle do not realize that the goal they have targeted is not the end but only the means to the end. For example, a man often sets out to become a millionaire simply because he has an inordinate fear of being poor. Having been made to feel rejected by society, he vows that he will never be poor again so that he won't ever again be at the mercy of those who could keep him in a "have-not" situation. Having been hurt once, he takes drastic measures never to be hurt again.

It would be impossible for such a person to protect himself on every front. While he is staving off society at large, he may be neglecting those closest to him within the family and wind up a lonely divorced man, sitting on a pile of money. His quest for acceptance through money and power ends up being the very thing that causes him to be rejected at home. Finding acceptance in one arena frequently guarantees rejection in another. A man may spend all of his waking hours to provide nice things for his family. In the end he may be shocked to realize how little his family appreciated his efforts. It seldom dawns on him until it is too late that his family would gladly have traded all the things he gave them for the time with him that he spent earning them. He had given them everything but himself.

Rejecting one's family to find acceptance in the marketplace or in compulsive church work is a poor trade. Many who are thus motivated do not have the foggiest notion that they are rejecting their families until family problems, divorce, or other tragedy strikes the home.

The Denver newspapers gave a brief account of the murder of a fifty-three-year-old company president and his wife from an affluent suburb of Dallas. Their fourteen-year-old son obviously had perceived rejection from them and retaliated with the ultimate in rejection—he murdered both of them.

Many spend their entire lives in the pursuit of a goal

only to find that attaining it gives no more than fleeting satisfaction. When this happens they must begin a new quest immediately. If the goal were true and meaningful, the one who achieves it could find some satisfaction from his success. But when the person doesn't understand that acceptance is the focal point of his search, he will need a succession of intermediate goals each of which, in their turn, will prove hollow victories. For example, a man may buy a new car and have, for a short time, a feeling of elation. However, after the new wears off the car, it no longer is a source of satisfaction and status.

The interminable quest for acceptance, however well defined or obscured, is indicative of the rejection syndrome having been in operation. The person who has known a series of childhood rejections usually has an emotional void which is craving fulfillment. Such a person constantly pursues acceptance or fulfillment, a mute testimony to the fact that rejection has caused the void. A teenaged girl or young woman may give her body to a succession of men for the momentary satisfaction of being accepted. However, she will find out sooner or later that only her body is being accepted while her person is being rejected.

The bottom line of the rejection syndrome is that a person who has been rejected will ultimately reject himself and, in turn, will reject others in the same way he has been rejected. Or, a rejected person may also overcompensate and treat others in an opposite manner to the way in which he was treated. For example, if he were deprived of love and affection, he may overreact by smothering his own children with overprotection, denying the children's personhood—which is another form of rejection.

It might be helpful to look briefly at the quest for acceptance and identity by age groups to see the powerful role they play in the full range of life experiences. To do so we will examine six categories: (1) Prenatal, (2) Childhood, (3) Youth, (4) Young Adulthood, (5) Middle Years, and (6) Mature Years.

THE PRENATAL PERIOD

Recent years have seen some advancements in research methods to help understand the physiological abnormalities which accrue to the fetus. Some abnormalities are as a result of genetics. Some of them are caused by stress the mother undergoes during pregnancy. Substance abuse, such as alcohol or street drugs, even prescribed medications such as Thalidomide, taken by the mother can cause damage to the unborn child. Research has also substantiated a cause-and-effect relationship between a mother's rejection of the unborn child and the psychological difficulties of the child in later life.

Rejection in its insipient stages or the prenatal imprints can be indelibly engraved into the makeup of the personality. Though it may be difficult to establish a one-to-one correspondence between events during pregnancy and particular personality traits, the generalized effects of emotional stress and tension in the mother can be readily discerned in the psychodynamics of the infant.

CHILDHOOD

Obviously, children naturally need and seek the acceptance of their parents. If they find their acceptance in a meaningful way, the children are free to engage in pursuits that are not totally self-centered and designed primarily to make them feel good about themselves. Such acceptance, coming about in a natural manner,

21

leaves them free to be motivated by positive rather than negative means. In other words, they are free to be spontaneous and creative because their love and acceptance needs have been met.

Everyone has witnessed children showing off or acting up, or otherwise participating in increasingly antisocial behavior to get attention. Another child may revert to infantile behavior in order to get some of the same attention.

Failure to get the desired acceptance eventually results in frustration and hostility, which the child may retain inside him or find some way to release. To put it another way, a child may "act in" or "act out." The child who is quiet and never gets into trouble is often considered a model child, while the one who is more honest and open in his displays of anger is branded as a troublemaker. The one who is withdrawn, quiet, and hurting has a problem equally as deep as the one who is releasing his symptoms. Both have the same problem— just a different method of expressing the symptoms. The child who keeps it all in may later develop somatic complaints (physical ailments) while the one who lets it all out may cause others to develop a few!

YOUTH

As a child begins to develop a personality separate and apart from his parents, he naturally gravitates to his peers for interpersonal relationships. If he has a healthy attitude toward himself, these new relationships will complement and supplement his continuing relationship with his parents.

A vacuum in the relationship with his parents will result in an inordinate dependence upon peers for acceptance and meaning. Being driven to find acceptance outside the family due to unhealthy or pathological conditions in the home can result in unwholesome liaisons, such as homosexual relations. When this kind of behavior has its roots in the very early years, it is not unusual to hear a person living a homosexual life-style say, "I have known I was different since I was four or five years of age." When this rationalization is accepted as fact, such a person may quit fighting it and accept the idea that he or she was born homosexual. Sadly, this deception finds much support within and without the "gay" community.

During this period of life, peer groups are common and such associations can be healthy for those who do not use them as their primary source of acceptance. Those who are driven to find acceptance from their peers are likewise driven to participate in behaviors which may range from antisocial to criminal as a means of earning or maintaining the acceptance they have found.

As a child grows to puberty and adolescence, the young person with a good self-concept will begin to establish an identity which will serve as a springboard to adulthood. Others will identify with a person or persons which may prove deleterious. Sports, music, and other such endeavors may not be harmful in themselves, but they can prove to be so if they are viewed as an end rather than a means.

A young man with whom I had a passing contact in a psychiatric ward was convinced that his face was grotesque. He was a handsome nineteen-year-old, tall and athletic. His basketball record in high school had earned him a full scholarship at a major university. For him, his identity and acceptance, as well as his future, hinged upon his ability as a basketball player. However, at the end of the season, he injured a knee and had to give up his scholarship. Sports had become his life and, without this, life had no meaning. He couldn't face what seemed an impossible situation and his method of handling it was to break with reality which resulted in thinking that his face was grotesque. A minor knee injury was all that it took to destroy his identity and his means of finding acceptance.

Some young people, knowing they can't make it in sports, turn to other activities, such as academic studies. If they do well, they may go on to achieve acceptance with graduate degrees. The identity established in childhood or youth frequently carries over into adulthood. There are many who never get finished with their education, from childhood through old age. What began as an escape becomes a prison from which they lack the courage to escape. Or, the circumstances which forced a retreat to academics might well be the means to propel such a person into a brilliant academic career.

YOUNG ADULTHOOD

The person who knows his calling in life spends much of this time in preparation and in becoming established, both in career and family. By contrast, the person who is insecure in his personhood finds it difficult to do either.

From my own personal experience, I know that my inferiority feelings as a teenager made it impossible for me to make a volitional choice to pursue a particular career. College was a muddled time. The degree program I selected was more by default than by choice.

Employment was obtained on a similar line and had little relationship to my four years of preparation. The next sixteen years were a period of frustration, discouragement, and defeat during which time my family was cheated by my lack of emotional energy. What should have been a time of becoming established in a career was actually a time of becoming increasingly enmeshed and entrenched in psychological and interpersonal difficulties.

I finally *arrived* at age thirty-five—I arrived *at the*

bottom! As the Holy Spirit revealed the reality of Galatians 2:20: "I am crucified with Christ . . . ," I found an acceptance and an identity based on something more realistic and permanent than my performance. This new acceptance and identity was foundational for my life's work which followed.

Some people are prepared by positive means; others are a little more obstinate and require considerable negative processing. I belonged to the latter group where I am joined by many others. It is not the recommended way, but the lessons learned in the "school of hard knocks" are not soon forgotten.

During the young adult years, identity and acceptance are frequently based on achievement. When the achievement is satisfactory, the good life may seem to be fulfilling for a period of time. However, the good life, as defined by the world in terms of materialism, just doesn't bring lasting satisfaction. It is really "the bad life," with a humanistic facade which makes it desirable to those who live to appease the lusts of the flesh.

MIDDLE YEARS

By the time a person reaches his forties, it begins to dawn upon him that he is going to make his goals, has already achieved them, or that the goals will never be realized. In either case, he is faced with an identity crisis which some call the mid-life crisis. Some would define this period in terms of physiological changes in both the male and the female. For the female, menopause is a physiological fact accompanied by hormonal and psychological ramifications. For the male, the psychological trauma may be just as great, though it has no basis in organic changes.

The man who has made his goals or has them in sight may see no meaningful frontiers to conquer like those to which he has been dedicated. Also, his physical strength may not allow him to invest as much of himself as he did. The goals he has already reached no longer provide a sense of accomplishment. A change of career may be out of the question for some people because of family responsibilities. Others will not sacrifice their pride to switch to a meaningful and fulfilling life of service to others because it does not pay as much, in money or prestige, as their old position.

A man during this time might bury himself in business, or turn to religion, or to women. One has only to observe those who have not found their identity and acceptance in Christ to validate this statement in the lives of people they know. When business or career goals are attained or unattainable, and the children have left the nest, extramarital affairs are becoming more and more common.

The mother who has no career outside the home may find her identity and meaning in her husband and children. Loss of her husband or her children growing up and leaving home can cause an identity crisis for her. Her reasons for living have just walked out of the house or died and left a vacuum which yearns for fulfillment. The identity which has been based on a role or interpersonal relationships is always subject to change without notice.

The feminist movement is producing a generation of women oriented to finding meaning in their roles outside the home in competition with men. Such competition has its liabilities as well as its assets. Stress-induced illnesses once more common to men are now showing up in women. Lung cancer due to smoking is more prevalent among women than it once was. Some women find competition with their husbands to be destructive to the marriage relationship.

Mothers who work outside the home, by necessity or by choice, are depriving their children of nurture which would be difficult to assess in terms of the rejection experienced by the children. The single-parent family almost always results in the mother working outside the home. This separation only adds to the trauma inflicted on the child by the breakup of the marriage.

Discouragement and defeat caused by failure to achieve temporal goals and the guilt resulting from the neglect of the family or from getting involved in extramarital relationships drive such people to find relief. Alcohol or drugs, prescribed or otherwise, may serve as a temporary expedient to dull the pain.

Pursuit of counterfeit solutions frequently results in suicide or half-hearted suicide attempts. Losing oneself in the lives of others, doting on a child or parent, may be a diversion to prevent some of them from working on their own problems.

The person who finds a succession of meaningful goals may live a fairly satisfying life and never come to know an identity which transcends this life. Someone who is devoted to others may be continually doing for others in order to find acceptance for himself. Another person may devote all available time and money for material things for his self-entertainment. Eventually, the lure and appeal of the toys wane and something else has to be found. For some it may even be the inordinate amount of time they spend preparing for retirement.

MATURE YEARS

Some barely limp into retirement, expecting to find solace in their escape from the rat race to enjoy the leisure Madison Avenue advertising has led them to believe lies ahead for them. Others retire with expectations based more on fantasy than reality.

They soon realize that they are "has beens." Those who developed a satisfactory identity based on achievement are no longer achievers, and those who have never achieved are remorseful about the past, dissatisfied with the present, and fearful about the future. The wisdom of the years is lost in the shuffle(board). True wisdom, which begins with the fear of God, has not ever had its proper place—at the beginning, middle, or at the end of their lives.

GENUINE IDENTITY AND ACCEPTANCE

A life based on temporal values, goals, and interpersonal relationships develops an identity and finds its acceptance in things and relationships that are fleeting at best. Identity and acceptance based on these result ultimately in rejection by others, and, finally self-rejection.

The best way to arrive at an understanding of the rejection syndrome is to live it vicariously through the lives of others. In the next chapter we will examine a wide range of rejection patterns seen in certain lives which were devastated by rejection in its many forms, with some of which you may be able to identify. Understanding the symptoms wrought by the rejection syndrome, however, is merely the prelude to isolating the problem and finding the only complete answer, which is in the Lord Jesus Christ.

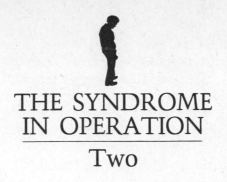

THE SYNDROME IN OPERATION
Two

In *The Ins and Out of Rejection*, I mentioned two basic types of rejection, overt and covert, or obvious and subtle. Some of the most damaging rejection by parents is of the latter type and is usually unintentional. Likewise, it is more frequently emotionally felt without being intellectually understood by the child.

SUBTLE REJECTION

The overt forms of rejection and the resulting emotional damage can easily be seen. However, rejection which takes place in subtle ways may create the same emotional havoc and not be so easily understood. It can happen in a number of ways.

Overprotection, or smothering, which prevents a child from becoming the fully functioning person he was intended to be.

Performance-based or *conditional love*, which says, "I love you *if*..." The if indicates that it is the performance which is being accepted rather than the person.

Premature death of parents, where the primary source

of love and acceptance is permanently lost.

Deprivation of parental love due to unavoidable conditions such as extended hospitalization in infancy or early childhood, or military service, is common.

The broken home where at least one of the parents does not have daily contact with the child is another form of rejection.

Inability of the parents to communicate their love to the child verbally, physically, or both, is another form of rejection.

Unfavorable comparison with other siblings, where favoritism is shown, is another form of subtle rejection.

These and a host of other behaviors and actions can result in a child's feeling rejection where none may be intended. Sometimes the parent's actions are totally unavoidable. Rejection, whether overt or covert, causes some degree of self-rejection resulting in a damage to the recipient's self-esteem. In turn, such a person will pass along rejection in some form, similar to or opposite to that which he sustained, to those with whom he has daily contact—especially to those whom he loves and those who love him.

We all experience rejection to one degree or another on a daily basis because conditional human love is always imperfect. The perfect unconditional love of God is the only love devoid of any taint of rejection. We experience this love through an understanding of our identity and acceptance in the Lord Jesus Christ, through death and resurrection with him. Even those who have found this relationship with him usually have already done some damage to their children.

Most of our personality traits are established by the time we are three and a half years to four years of age. In God's plan, damage done during this time is not irreversible, but it means the personality will need to be restructured through the renewing of the mind by the

Holy Spirit. As a person is filled with the Holy Spirit, and enters into all that is his in Christ, many behavior patterns and feelings can be miraculously changed.

Understanding the negative effects of rejection upon the personality is not in itself curative. In fact, understanding is not even the problem. The rejection syndrome in action is merely indicative of a deeper issue—the self-centered life that has yet to be dealt with by the Holy Spirit. Many spend a lifetime trying to cope and compensate for what is missing, spending thousands of dollars on different forms of therapy to aid them in the process. If they are successful, they have only better adjusted flesh or self-life. The symptoms may be better but the self-life has been enhanced rather than being dealt with by the Cross. Unless the Cross (co-death and co-resurrection with Christ) becomes a reality through the Spirit's revelation, the problem, the entrenched self-life, is worsened even as the symptoms are assuaged.

This is not to say that therapy has no value from a human standpoint. Nor is it correct to say that all psychological problems are sin problems. Relief of certain symptoms may prevent suicide or other damaging behaviors. However, dealing with the psychological issues without resolving a person's spiritual problems gives a psychological boost that can hurt the person spiritually. Frequently, extreme psychological problems are the very means God uses to accomplish the brokenness that makes the person ready for the Cross experience.

An understanding of the syndrome is a helpful, though not vital, tool in assessing the flesh and the "defense mechanisms" which unwittingly have been used to avoid the Cross. These compensatory behaviors may be sin or they may be just socially and religiously acceptable means through which a person finds comfort and meaning.

The fact that the genesis of such behavior, thinking, or feeling may be traced to past rejection in no way exonerates anyone from personal responsibility. It does provide a reasonable explanation for why one person reacts one way and another person in exactly the opposite way, even among siblings who have the same parents. The treatment parents may give to each of their children could be drastically different, depending upon the circumstances. The first child may have been born before the parents became Christians. The second could have had Christian parents during his formative years who were overactive in church work. The third may have been born after the parents had experienced the abundant or exchanged life and whose ministry accorded with their spiritual gifts.

The parents of the children were the same people, but, in a real sense, each of the children experienced their parents in a different set of circumstances. The same occurs when the family circumstances change from child to child even though the parents may have been Christians prior to marriage. Unstable situations caused by parents being yet in college, frequent relocations due to employment, health conditions of a parent, and a host of other situations could result in siblings experiencing a different world while being in the same home.

The psychological symptoms developed within the child as he matures could be due to overt sin on his part or that of his parents, but it would be hard to prove that all untoward behavior can be traced to overt sin. Ultimately, sin (through Adam) can be blamed for *all* of our problems, and Satan is the undisputed author of this power of sin in the world. Using this rationale, an individual could justify any kind of behavior by saying, "The devil made me do it." But we would all agree that we can't deny personal responsibility that easily.

Even though a person may have been, from his earliest

childhood days, programmed emotionally to reject and be rejected, he can not avoid culpability for his sins. By examining the rejection syndrome, we are not negating personal responsibility but promoting increased understanding of the damage that has taken place to the emotions as a result of rejection.

Many people have found great relief in the knowledge that they are not responsible for damage sustained to their emotions prior to their conscious memory or in early childhood. They may have added layer upon layer of emotional "scar tissue" by their unprofitable and sinful behavior, but the initial emotional programming was totally beyond their control, both as to its source and their reactions to it in infancy and early childhood.

Once the syndrome and the antidote—forgiveness of sins and knowing Christ as the source of new life—are understood, the individual has total responsibility for the sins he commits. He is also responsible for permitting these damaged emotions to continue uncontrolled.

The life lived in the power of the flesh will bear some of the earmarks of past rejection experiences. Positive, even scriptural, behavior may come and negative and sinful behavior may go; but the self-centered self-life, the life operating on its own resources, is ever more firmly entrenched until the exchanged life, the life that is under the dominion and power of the Holy Spirit, becomes an experiential reality. It is possible for Christians to be deceived into thinking that putting on scriptural behavior results in putting off a carnal or fleshly life. Such a person is really *doing* in order to *be* rather than *being* in order to *do*.

Rejection has its influence throughout all stages of life and on all of life's goals and relationships. The experiences and testimonies that follow will show how the rejection syndrome has taken its toll and also how God has transformed some lives by showing them their acceptance in Christ.

PRENATAL IMPRINTS

Frequently adults say that what happened to them in childhood has nothing to do with their adult lives. In doing so, they disclaim any relationship between negative experiences as a child and negative attitudes about themselves in adult life. More rare is the person who sees the relationship between the psychological state of the mother and the fetus. A relaxed, happy mother is much more likely to have a contented baby than a mother who is nervous and insecure. The circumstances surrounding the birth and the stability of the family are major determinants of the psychological well-being of the new baby.

Some years ago I counseled with a mother who had been in extreme psychological stress during her pregnancy. When the baby was born she was told that he had an ulcer. Before and after birth, the baby is impacted positively by love, warmth, and security, or negatively by the absence of these ingredients so vital to his emotional stability.

THE UNWANTED CHILD

One of the most common causes for rejection of a child prior to its birth and afterward is that it was unplanned and unwanted. Somehow the fetus picks up the mother's emotions and the rejection signals that she is sending. Mothers have told me that such children had rejected them from birth and refused to be cuddled and held. Somehow, rejection was sensed and returned.

A woman who was counseled some years ago remembers being told by her parents that they didn't want her. In her early childhood she remembers climbing a tree and trying to determine how she could be unborn. Her life history was one of rejecting and being rejected, which finally brought her in for counseling.

There are many reasons why a child may be unwanted.

A common reason, of course, is that the mother is unmarried. If the mother gets married to legitimatize the baby or "give it a name," the child may feel, or even be told, that he or she was the cause of the marriage and the untold misery which followed. Not only does the child feel that his or her appearance was a mistake; but also, the child may feel the burden of holding the parents together—a great responsibility for a child to assume.

The child who is unwanted may be given away through adoption at birth, which is an obvious form of rejection. Not only does the child suffer from the rejection but from the identity problem of not knowing who he or she really is. To compound the issue, the adoptive parents frequently have waited for years to have a child, and when they finally get one, they smother the child with love and wind up overprotecting it, thus giving it another form of rejection.

The reader may have difficulty in seeing how overprotection, whether or not it is a result of adoption, is really a form of rejection. On the surface it would seem that the terms are mutually exclusive. However, the child who has too many decisions made for him is receiving an underlying message which the parents usually do not realize they are sending. The unspoken message goes something like this: "You're too dumb to make good decisions; we have the wisdom so we will make all decisions for you."

When a child receives such treatment for a number of years, it is logical that he should feel inferior and lack confidence in his own decisions. To put it another way, when a child is not allowed or taught to *become* a person, he has been rejected *as* a person. Such a child may have many conflicting emotions—negative feelings toward the natural parents and ambivalence toward the overprotective adoptive parents. He loves his overprotective and/or adoptive parents for what they do for him and resents them for what they do to him. Over-protection or smothering is such a subtle form of rejection that the child then feels guilty for resenting such loving, wonderful parents, who seem outwardly to have nothing but his best interests at heart. The more he resents them, the more he resents himself for harboring resentment without just cause, a cause that he can't explain. His problem is compounded when he looks at his adoptive parents and cannot establish in them his roots or identity because he knows they are not his natural parents. Then he feels guilty if he seeks to locate his natural parents because he loves his adoptive parents and doesn't want to "betray" them.

When the unwanted child is kept by the natural parents, he may suffer false guilt all of his life. When he knows that he was an "accident," he may feel guilty for being born. This was hardly any of his doing, though he may be constantly blamed or reminded of his reponsibility. Any time a fight takes place between his parents, he may feel responsible for it. This guilt feeling can affect his daily life as an adult so that he feels as if he is occupying someone else's space, or driving in someone else's lane, or breathing someone else's air.

The false guilt may carry over into his Christian experience and he will confuse this false or imaginary guilt with guilt caused by sin. He may launch on an interminable journey of confessing sin and finding no relief. He may continually have problems with assurance of his salvation due to feeling unsaved.

The poor self-concept and the corresponding inferiority feelings will all but broadcast the message: "Please reject me; I'm so worthy of it." Those with whom he comes into contact will quickly pick up on the message and give him just the rejection which he seems so ardently to be seeking.

A child may get a double measure of rejection because he is not only unwanted but unlovely in appearance.

One such case caused a whole family to get involved with a rejection pattern. The father didn't want another child but he got one who he thought was the ugliest child he had ever seen. He rejected the child on both counts, which upset the mother terribly. One of the older children had compassion on the baby because of the father's rejection so the father rejected her as well. Then another child wanted acceptance from the father so he rejected both siblings to be on his father's side. The mother loved them all but just couldn't pull the act together for the whole family.

One of my former clients, whom we will call Tom, was a classic example of an overprotected child. He was born the second of three children in a midwestern farm family. His father was the oldest of ten children born to Swedish immigrants. His paternal grandfather was a harsh, demanding person who unknowingly broke his son's spirit (will) very early in his life.

Tom's mother lost her mother through death before she was three years old, and spent her early life in several foster home situations. She grew up a very strong-willed child who had to fend for herself through difficult circumstances. So both of his parents had known rejection from their earliest days. Typical of rejected people, they found each other and married.

Their first child was very strong-willed and energetic. The second child, Tom, was sensitive, fearful, and cried a lot. Very early he was weakened by a severe influenza infection which brought on bronchitis and later bronchial asthma. During this time, Tom's mother began to overprotect him, often keeping him out of school. She made all the decisions for him, not allowing him to do anything physically demanding. This overprotection continued through grade school, high school, and beyond.

Meanwhile, Tom's father, a hard-working, honest, and moral man, knew nothing about being loving and tender. He demanded hard work from his children, but never told Tom that he had done a good job. Tom longed to please his father or have his father praise him, but it never came. Even at thirty and forty years old, Tom was still trying to please his father but was never able to do so.

Tom always looked up to his older brother, dogged his tracks everywhere he went. His brother was a born leader while Tom was a born follower. The arrangement worked out well; but because he was so inept, his older brother often called Tom a dummy, an idiot, or stupid, which amounted to rejection. During later life Tom still looked up to his brother, but consistently felt inferior to him.

His mother's rejection was a classic example of overprotection while his father's and brother's was overt rejection. As a result, from the time Tom was in his twenties his life became one big performance treadmill—wanting desperately to do things that would make him acceptable to people, without fully understanding why. His singing career began in his twenties, spanned nearly twenty-five years, and was psychologically one big quest for acceptance. He knew God had given him a good voice and he did want to sing for God's glory, but lurking just under the surface was an unquenchable need for acceptance.

As a pastor in his middle and late thirties, Tom began to realize that something was wrong with him, but didn't know what. He had a fairly active social life but the romance that was to culminate in marriage never came along. He wanted women to like him, yet when one began to fall for him he would break it off and severely reject her, saying that she just was not the Lord's will for him.

At age forty Tom began to read some of Paul Tournier's books, from which he began to find great comfort in that they made him aware of what his problem was. But he didn't find concrete answers.

During the next ten years his perfectionist quest for acceptance grew. He would write and rew... each of his sermons two or three times, practice them several times in his study until his exciting messages helped him become a popular preacher. His church almost tripled in size during those years, but finally his drive caused him to burn out. One Sunday he entered the pulpit and couldn't even make the morning announcements. His voice just quit working. His ministry went downhill, and he was under the care of two different Christian psychiatrists, both of whom told him he should leave the ministry permanently.

Finally, he was recommended to Grace Fellowship where he learned about the rejection syndrome as the source of his symptoms as well as finding the solution to his problem (the self-life) in Christ. The transformation resulted in being restored to ministry and gave him also, with his new life, a wife.

OVERPROTECTION

Jim was in a double bind. His mother was overprotective and effusive in her expressions of "love" while his father could not express the genuine love he had. He was youngest in the family by several years, being born when his mother was around forty.

His mother had a difficult pregnancy and delivery, which merely added to her consternation at having another child at a late age. When Jim had a need as a child, his mother directed him to the older siblings to care for him. His mother was in complete control of him. He soon discovered that his only resource which couldn't be subverted was his mind. No one knew he was using it to prompt their interference.

As he grew into adulthood he found that he was unable to translate into practical work the things his mind could easily conceive. He couldn't even perform a minor task with hand tools, so his home was literally becoming a disaster area.

His mother continually said she loved him but he felt a different message coming through. Though he never was able to verbalize his feelings prior to counseling, his actions indicated that if what he was getting was love, he didn't need it. On the other hand, he was experiencing something nameless but pleasant between himself and his father. Only after his father died during the term of the counseling did he realize that it was love he had been feeling.

His mother said that she loved him, but it didn't communicate; his father communicated love, but couldn't articulate it. As a result, when his wife expressed love to him he couldn't accept it and became frustrated. They went through stormy times until Jim learned to accept love, first and foundationally from God, and then from his wife and others.

Anita was reared as an only child of special parents, who always meant the best in her upbringing. A common mistake with an only child, her parents overprotected her, which did not allow her to become a fully functioning person.

As Anita grew, she searched for love in different places. She was always liked by boys but because of inner conflicts and continuous introspection she did not relate as she wanted to with the girls in school, except for one lasting and precious friendship.

Still searching, she went into nurse's training for a few months in an attempt to satisfy her innermost longings. During this time she was engaged to a tall, handsome, proud young man. He was in the marines, and when he came home his attitudes had changed and again she saw her search unfulfilled. The engagement was broken and she went to another state where she stayed for one year and met another handsome young man and became engaged. After living in California, she soon realized this wasn't the answer, so she returned to her home state. Though she had been "the prodigal living in a far country," her parents took her back in and didn't cease to love her.

Reared a Catholic, she would go into the church when no one was there and pour out her heart to God, searching for answers. She talked as if she already knew God, but really didn't.

Before too long, she met another handsome young man and married him. They were married ten years and had two beautiful children before they were divorced.

Alex, her former husband, became involved with a woman with evil powers five years before the divorce and couldn't break loose from her. Anita saw him many times as a pale, driven man, aging at a rate beyond his years as he turned away from her. In addition to the psychological trauma this caused her, there was a variety of what appeared to be demonic manifestations. She found the simplest task difficult to perform.

Anita came to my wife and me for counseling when she was still in her seemingly interminable search. She began to find help when she knelt in my office and asked God's forgiveness for all her sins and then asked that Jesus come into her heart. Three months later she entered into the reality of her relationship with Christ. She began to see more clearly into the lifetime of damaged emotions. As she learned to walk in Christ she began to see how all her past rejections had led her to such a point of despair.

THE HANDICAPPED CHILD

When a child is brain damaged or retarded it is frequently very difficult for a parent to accept the handicap. One or both parents, rejecting the handicap, in doing so may reject the child. Or, the parents may be able to accept the child despite the condition, but the child becomes the butt of jokes and mockery by other children on the school ground and experiences rejection there.

It is not infrequent that handicapped children are overprotected and not allowed to develop to their full potential. When the parents do not have a healthy attitude toward the handicap and the child, the child picks up on it and develops unhealthy attitudes toward himself.

A lady was counseled who had been in leg braces due to polio as a very small child. She said her earliest memories could be summed up in one word—alienation. All during her childhood she had felt guilty for depriving her parents and siblings financially, since all available money had to be spent on doctors, hospitals, and braces. Although she obviously did not intentionally contract polio, her life was a continual "guilt trip" for being a burden on her family.

The handicapped also may be the occasion for other siblings being rejected. A Christian psychiatrist, on the board of directors for Grace Fellowship, Dr. Paul Kaschel, was the product of such a situation. Both his older and younger brothers were victims of cerebral palsy.

His mother had her hands full taking care of two handicapped sons in the home. Paul was normal, so he could take care of himself and received little of his mother's attention. His father, on the other hand, was busy in business and active in the Lord's work so Paul received very little of his time. As a senior in high school Paul achieved the name of being the most bashful person in a class of 250 students. He had no choice. He was driven to become a physician to establish a viable identity.

After he had firmly entrenched himself as a physician, surgeon, and then psychiatrist, he discovered the emptiness of an identity that was not, first of all, based on his relationship with Jesus Christ. Also, he had to face the fact that he had passed along rejection in its various forms to his wife and children. Finding his identity and acceptance in Christ transformed his life and gave him a ministry in his practice.

"Rejection was a word that was not in my vocabulary," said one of my clients whom we shall call Ruth. Yet, that was one of the problems she was experiencing. Ruth had polio as a child but had been brought up as normally as possible, despite braces and, later, a wheelchair. She grew up with the usual aches and pains of other children but felt totally accepted until her family moved after her seventh grade. She was double promoted in school so she was younger than her classmates. That had never been an issue before, but it became a real problem in the new situation. She began to feel rejected both at school and church.

The years through junior high and high school were very difficult. She was saved at a very young age, but began to feel that God took care of her father, a minister, but not her. Thirty years later, she began to realize the degree of rejection which had occurred during those years and the crippling effect it had on her emotionally, even as the polio had affected her physically. She never really talked to anyone because she felt it was God's will for her family to be there in the new location and, unconsciously, she felt as a person that she didn't really matter. Her father had, in essence, by his full-time availability to others, rejected his family by doing what he felt the Lord expected of him as a pastor. That was the beginning of her feelings of rejection by God.

In college she received more acceptance, and after graduation she went into the work world gaining executive status mostly in her own strength. Still she felt no genuine acceptance, and certainly, no "abundant life." She came in for counseling where she was confronted with a tremendous amount of anger and hostility that she had been unable to admit or resolve. After several months of praying and reading about the effects of rejection, and the answer, identification with Christ, the Lord began to show her that her main problem was the self-life and its outgrowth, her feelings of rejection. She made some progress in allowing the Lord to meet her needs. After struggling with that for about a year she finally did come to the end of herself and allow the truth of Galatians 2:20 to become experiential in her life.

THE SICKLY CHILD

Sickness or disease can have a lasting emotional impact on a child. In infancy, loving and cuddling a child can literally mean the difference between life and death. In one study done in Asia, infants received exactly the same care except some were shown acceptance by being held regularly, given plenty of tender loving care. The other group was not. Some of those who did not receive love actually died as a result.

Karen, a lady in her mid-twenties, was born prematurely and spent the first three months of her life in an incubator. Thus, the machine became her "mother." She had a difficult time when this "thing" with arms pawed at her when her mother took her home.

She was twenty-three years old before she could accept the fact that either of her parents loved her. She was a wanted child, the firstborn, and much loved by her parents. And yet, her isolation made her to feel totally rejected during the first three months, through no fault of anyone. They did the most loving thing that could possibly have been done but the emotional perception of the child was exactly the opposite. It took Karen twenty-five years to understand fully why she spurned her parents' love and why she found difficulty in relating to her husband.

PREMATURE DEATH OF PARENTS

The death of a parent or parents can have a lifelong impact on a young person. The sudden withdrawal of love, which is not replaced, or which is replaced with defective love, causes varied reactions.

Jill's father died when she was two years of age, leaving an emotional vacuum. A few years later her mother remarried. Jill did not feel the love from her stepfather which would meet her need to feel wanted and accepted. She probably resented this man's efforts to replace her father whom she loved deeply, and he may have resented Jill's intrusion into his relationship with her mother.

Other children came along, which also served to siphon off the love her stepfather might have given to Jill. Consciously or unconsciously, she made the decision very early that men would let her down if she let them get close. The first one had, and the rest probably would, too. As she grew older, she competed with men and set her goals to excel without them. Her fear of rejection was sufficiently in evidence to force her to keep men in their proper place—out of her life.

Needless to say, it is difficult to get married with such a personality profile. She was single in her early thirties. Through counseling she realized what she was doing to herself and entered into a new relationship with Christ and is now ready for God's choice, either to be married or remain single.

Ken, a fifteen-year-old, at six years of age had lost his father and brother in an auto accident. Four other close relatives died in the same year. The trauma of losing so many loved ones was like receiving a great rejection, which is best characterized as a loss of love. In counseling he was challenged to yield all that he was and had to the Lord Jesus Christ. Referring to all the defense mechanisms he used, he replied, "I've spent nine years building all of this up and I can't let go of it." He literally grabbed his abdomen and asked, "Do you have an antacid tablet?"

It was as though he had been stabbed in the stomach when he realized what giving it all up would mean. It seemed to him that he would just collapse in a little pile if he let go of his masterful job of holding his own life together. To my knowledge, he has yet to let go.

PARENTAL SUICIDE

At age sixteen, Shirley found her father's body in a thicket—the victim of a self-inflicted shotgun blast. Suicide, the most selfish act a person can perform, is the epitome of rejection. The person is saying, in effect, "I don't care what happens to anyone else. I'm going to take care of me."

Shirley could not cry at her father's death and had her first breakdown at age eighteen. The next came at age thirty, at which time she began twenty years of psychiatric treatment. She had ten years of private treatment and then ten years in and out of hospitals for varying lengths of time. She ran the entire gamut of treatment regimes, all to no avail. For the last ten years she was on heavy tranquilizers every day and sleeping pills at night.

During this time she alienated her children, who threatened never to set foot in the home again. She threatened suicide on a regular basis and her husband had to leave work innumerable times to see if she was still alive. At the time God met her in 1970, she was down to skin and bones and her husband said she literally could no longer write her own name. One weekend the Holy Spirit worked in her life, showing her how to overcome this overwhelming sense of rejection by receiving Christ's love and acceptance and subsequently the love of her husband and children.

Within a month she no longer needed tranquilizers

or sleeping pills and within three months she had gained back seventeen pounds and her health. Since that time she has been vitally involved in sharing with others how the Spirit of God can permanently release them from mental and emotional disturbances.

BROKEN HOMES

A young man was hurt deeply when his parents divorced shortly before his teen years. He was forced to earn his way almost from that point onward. During his teenage years a customer where he worked led him to Christ and continued to show a personal interest in him.

Called to the ministry, he worked his way through Bible college and threw himself into dedicated serving and was greatly used of the Lord. From the beginning, he had a gnawing hunger for something but he didn't know what. He searched diligently for an answer to his internal turmoil. He would go to his office as if on an errand and would stay and pray and weep for hours but no answer came. He attended seminars, conferences, and anything else which might offer a ray of hope.

His wife of more than twenty years affirmed that he was the best preacher she had ever heard. The church continued to multiply and all of the signs of success were in evidence. He finally found a means of assuaging the torment within—acceptance through a series of affairs. Eventually, one of the women confessed to what was happening and the pastor left town with his family the same day. His wife's unswerving faithfulness prevented his breaking with reality as he had known it. His coming into true reality, acceptance in the Lord Jesus Christ, showed him the only complete answer to his insatiable hunger for unconditional love.

Another man from exactly the same background reacted much differently. He, too, was unwanted by his parents and was on his own from age twelve. He was married in his midteens and had a daughter to whom he could show no love. He was saved at twenty-one and began to be able to show some affection to his daughter, who still suffers the effects of his inability to show love. The child's mother died from tuberculosis shortly after the little girl's birth.

When the girl was still very young, her father remarried and had another family, all of whom suffered rejection by him. He was a Hebrew and Greek scholar who spent his entire life in the pastoral ministry, planting churches and winning many people to Christ. In his late sixties he had several coronaries, all of which could be attributed to a lifetime of emotional conflict.

As he understood the effects of rejection in his life and the lives of those around him, he was able also to appropriate Christ's love and acceptance, and found victory over the effects of rejection. However, he also felt the heartache of now having an answer which he had been unable to find which would have provided help for himself and other hurting persons he had encountered in his lifetime of ministry.

Jane's parents divorced when she was ten years old, just one of many childhood experiences that made her feel different from others her age. She wanted to be accepted but felt she never could be because she was "different." She accepted Christ when she was thirteen, but not understanding how to live the Christian life, she was left to flounder on her own. First she tried being good, but discovered how often she fell short of the goals. She began then to hate herself for being so bad, thinking she was the ugliest person ever to live and that she would never be able to do anything right. She felt like a nobody, a worthless person. She finally accepted her lot in life as a Christian so unworthy that she must "suffer" for Jesus. Even though she wanted people to like her and accept her, she thought it would never happen.

Her most secret hopes and desires seemed to be coming true when she met Jim and they were married. Jim made her feel like the girl in the fairy tale who had married the handsome prince. But the ending wasn't "happily ever after." The marriage seemed so beautiful for the first few years—with both wanting the marriage to be what God wanted it to be. They read books, went to seminars, and talked about the roles and priorities of the family. Jim took a full-time Christian job. They had four children within six years. There seemed so much to do. They were burdened for the lost and for those in need. People seemed to accept Jane when she did things for Jim's ministry at the church. She became a compulsive worker, striving to win the acceptance of others, but she took her work to an extreme. Reaching the limits of her abilities, she became frustrated and upset and could not keep up the pace. She withdrew from her endless activities and turned to Jim looking for fulfillment in her life. Jim was so involved with the church that he couldn't see her needs and became unresponsive to her. She gradually became distant from him and after thirteen years of marriage she no longer felt love for him. Life seemed so unbearable to her and the marriage seemed hopeless. She wanted a divorce, though she had hated the very sound of the word since she was a child. Feeling there was nothing left for which to live for she prayed to die.

Her husband Jim was a very capable person with natural leadership talents. As a result he found his own strength sufficient to accomplish nearly everything he had ever attempted. Reliance on his own strength persisted into his Christian work. He sought to serve God, but in his own strength. His self-image was tied to his position as a people-helper, to feeling indispensable, so he bred dependency on himself into those with whom he ministered. People found it hard to wean themselves away from him. He didn't clearly perceive this dynamic, but the burden of dependent people became a growing problem in his ministry, his marriage, and his personal life. He was always the teacher, helper, counselor, but never close friend to anyone. He thought that letting others know his weaknesses would interfere with his serving them. His wife was no exception to this dynamic, and she gradually felt more and more unnecessary to him, which amounted to further rejection for her, and she turned to an affair in an attempt to find acceptance.

Jim quickly rose to leadership roles, authored two books before age thirty, and was president of an interdenominational ministry. Several years ago he accepted the pastor-teacher role in an innovative church. As the church grew, the dynamics of his ministry created an increasing load on his shoulders. He lost his joy and strength under the load and the ministry began to break him. The combination of ministry impotence and marriage breakdown broke him as a person.

Jim saw the crisis as God's way for forcing him to stop depending on his own strength and capabilities. As he began to rest in Christ, allowing him to live through him, God began to heal their lives.

Jane was also convicted of her sin and her self-centered attempts to live the Christian life in her own strength. She dealt with her sin and began to allow Christ to live his life through her. When she was freed from the constant struggle within her to attain self-sufficiency and acceptance through other people, the restoration of their marriage and forgiveness of their church has resulted in multiplied ministry by both Jim and Jane.

HOMOSEXUALITY

A sixteen-year-old boy had been rejected by his father, but found acceptance by a pastor. The acceptance meant so much that the boy decided to become a minister, a choice which could have easily been predicted. The minister was elated that he had a budding minister in his congregation and shepherded him to the local Bible college to look it over with a view that he attend there. After the visit the young man decided against the ministry, and the pastor dropped him like a hot potato. For the young man it was just one more rejection.

The young man later married and had children, but he never found the acceptance which he had sought all of his life. In his late thirties, he and his wife had invited a friend to spend a few days with them while the friend was becoming situated in a new job and was looking for an apartment.

For the first time, the man who had known so much rejection found unconditional acceptance with another person and entered into a homosexual affair with his friend, leaving his wife and children. The acceptance met a need that he had not known how to allow the Lord Jesus Christ to meet.

SUMMARY

These examples of rejection are by no means exhaustive. This small sampling, however, may serve to show some concrete illustrations of how rejection occurs and how interpersonal relationships are negatively affected, if not destroyed.

The divorce rate is mute testimony to rejection taking place between husband and wife, resulting in the final rejection in the divorce courts. When each looks for needs to be met and hurts to be healed by the mate rather than in the Lord Jesus Christ, the impossible dream often becomes a nightmare of rejecting and being rejected.

It is impossible to live in the world without experiencing rejection. Apart from Christ it is not possible to find the kind of acceptance which nullifies the psychological damage rejection causes. Not only does God accept the lost through the death of Christ for our sins but he also manifests his unconditional acceptance to us by revealing the untold power available to us through our union with Christ in his death and resurrection.

Anyone who has realized the significance of what rejection at the hand of others has done to mar the past should understand also how the revelation of acceptance in Christ can transform the life in the present and open up a glorious future.

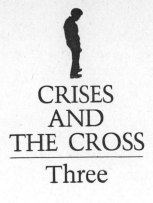

CRISES
AND
THE CROSS
Three

A crisis can be a bane or a blessing. It can either make a
person bitter or better. A satisfied person in a humdrum
routine sees no cause for changes in his life-style. If the
humdrum routine is not satisfying, however, a crisis
may be precipitated deliberately to break the monotony.

Since we are, by nature, resistant to change, it usually
takes a crisis to force reevaluation of the presupposi-
tions upon which we base our lives. We often just
permit life to happen and adopt the standards of those
around us rather than come to grips with who we are,
what we do, and why.

Many believers find it easier to live out an assigned
identity with a ready-made set of standards, even if it is
less than satisfying, than to question the foundations
upon which they base their lives and life choices. In
fact, it is considered almost sinful, even heretical, to
challenge the underpinnings of one's belief systems.
Such believers choose a church and Christian friends
with whom they agree about what is right and wrong to
do. Following the agreed-upon rules and avoiding the
taboos qualify them as "good Christians." Often they
never question the ready-made standards and life-style

of the group, though such a life of self-effort may offer very little personal meaning.

When life lived in one's own strength, as described above, becomes no longer tolerable, the believer searches to find something which does give meaning. Eventually, it will be discovered that it is not *something* or even *many things* which give meaning. The believer may then resort to activities to fill the void. The seeking and searching believer may dedicate his life to service or to the standards of some church or organization. When he conforms to these standards, he is rewarded with acceptance, which can be extremely meaningful. The service rendered to the Lord is also satisfying as he sees spiritual results taking place in others as a result. But even this dedicated service, done in the strength of the flesh, may eventually end in disillusionment if not in total defeat.

On the other hand, a believer who is steeped in legalism (in seeking acceptance by God and others based on what he does), may become increasingly disenchanted with the demands placed on him and the meager results of his service. He may give up such a strict life-style and become involved in a less demanding form of Christianity to find freedom or to become involved in a life of sin, or both. When the power of the flesh has been forcibly restrained for a long period of time, it is not at all unusual for it to explode in a display of blatant immorality.

Trying too hard or not trying at all are both self-effort, but it is the performance that wins the praise of man. The goals and methods may be different, but neither the active nor the passive receives the full blessing of God.

The quest for acceptance, the praise of God and man, and a meaningful identity must ultimately result in frustration when they are sought in service for the Lord

Jesus rather than through abiding in him, with service being the result. Working for acceptance and an identity based on self-effort goes on both inside and outside the church, with the same unfulfilling results.

An overemphasis on obedience or law at the expense of grace results in legalism; an overemphasis on grace at the expense of obedience results in passivity, if not license. When people seek acceptance in other people instead of in the Lord Jesus, some degree of rejection is inevitable, since it is impossible to please everyone. Likewise, an identity based on performance is like trying to please God by keeping the law rather than by receiving unconditional acceptance and identity based on his unconditional grace. For that reason the comparison of law and grace as they are taught in the Bible, is extremely appropriate in understanding identity and acceptance.

Identity and acceptance based on performance (under law) necessitate the proper feedback from others which leads to bondage. Identity and acceptance in Christ (grace) leads to acceptance from others as well.

It is the lack of understanding of scriptural identity and acceptance that forces the believer to attempt the establishment of a counterfeit system to meet his own needs, and he often even seeks God to help him do so. By these efforts he sets himself up for an inevitable clash between the two systems as he finds it increasingly difficult to sustain identity and acceptance in his own strength. Failure to find meaning and acceptance over a period of time may result in bankruptcy, not just financial and professional, but mental, emotional, in interpersonal and in family relationships.

The breakdown comes when the need is recognized and a solution becomes mandatory. Either there will be a revision of the system or the adoption of an entirely new system. The *flesh* was spoken of by the Apostle

Paul as a function or condition of our soul, the part of our personality that strives through self-effort to control our lives. The flesh, being what it is, keeps trying one revision after another until presented with an insoluble crisis. When the truth of acceptance and identity in Christ is presented at this precise point, the exchange of the self-life for the Christ-life is the only way out.

All too frequently, it is only in retrospect that the believer is able to appreciate why God has allowed the crisis to come.

THE PURPOSE OF CRISES

Although it is not God's will that the believer just live from crisis to crisis, it is often the life pattern for some of his children. Some people take advantage of crises to get thrills, to relieve monotony, or to draw attention to themselves. The Apostle John wrote, expressing the desire of the heavenly Father's heart: "I have no greater joy than to hear that my children walk in the truth" (3 John 4). The believer who is consistently walking in truth will not need crises to force him back to reliance upon the Father and to walk in the Spirit. Or, to put it another way, when a life of holiness is being lived, chastening is unnecessary.

Crises are for the purpose of chastening or teaching us that we might draw nigh to God and walk in truth. Hebrews 12:10 concludes that chastening is used in our lives "that we might be partakers of his holiness." Sometimes the crisis involves someone else, as a sick child may be used to draw its mother back to reliance upon God.

All kinds of crises may present themselves during our spiritual sojourn, but underlying all of them is the issue of identity. Crises prove in a practical manner whether our identity is based upon temporal and external things, or whether we are more interested in how the situation affects us or anyone else. Paul wrote: "But what things were gain to me, those I counted loss for Christ. Yea, doubtless, and I count all things but loss for the excellency of the knowledge of Christ Jesus my Lord: for whom I have suffered the loss of all things, and do count them but dung, that I may win Christ, and be found in him, not having mine own righteousness, which is of the law, but that which is through the faith of Christ, the righteousness which is of God by faith: That I may know him, and the power of his resurrection, and the fellowship of his sufferings, being made conformable unto his death" (Philippians 3:7-10).

Suffering loss usually is a crisis, whether it be a loss of possessions or personal acceptance. The first has more to do with our identity, while the loss of love or personal acceptance, as in death or divorce, has greater impact on our worth or self-esteem. Identity is the manner in which we relate to ourselves while acceptance, or the lack of it, depends on the relationship with those meaningful persons around us. A pastor's wife who becomes a widow has lost the role which gave her identity to the extent that she found her meaning through her husband and the position he held.

An identity based on things or accomplishments may suffice for varying lengths of time, but ultimately it will fail to satisfy unless it brings a degree of acceptance from other people whom we consider as significant.

Though a crisis may have no apparent connection with identity, our response to it reveals the values which we consider important. For example, a loss of money or material things can make us or break us. A person whose entire identity is based upon what he has will be completely destroyed by the loss of all things.

Acceptance, likewise, has much to do with our identity. When acceptance is sought on a temporal level, many of the crisis experiences during a lifetime will involve fractured relationships, which are serious blows to self-esteem. Human relationships are fleeting, all of them ending in death, either ours or the other person's. Without the vital spiritual dimension, such relationships are inherently selfish on both parts. When the expectations upon which relationships are built are not fulfilled on the part of one or both persons, a rupture occurs in the relationship, producing a crisis. Its impact will be directly proportional to the investment in the relationship and the quality of past relationships. And to that degree the identity of the person or persons involved will be affected.

Whether identity is based on the relationship with things or people, the total loss of either can present a crisis of life and death proportions. When the reason for living is lost, some at that moment elect death by their own hand.

When identity is based on temporal things or relationships, when these are lost, all is lost. When identity is based on who we are in the Lord Jesus Christ, we can, with Paul, suffer the loss of all things and still survive, or better yet, ". . . count it all joy" (James 1:2).

The chastening or discipline which God permits to test or try us is another form of crisis. These crises can be friends that bring us to the place of spiritual maturity and of walking according to truth. We will either walk in truth about who we are in Christ or we will, to our detriment, walk in some false path, seeking identity. It is through chastening that we experience a variety of crises and become "partakers of his holiness" and experience "the peaceable fruit of righteousness" (Hebrews 12:11).

God will faithfully teach us through the Word and guide us into all the truth. It is in experiencing some of the "all things" crises of Romans 8:28 that we are brought into the glorious privilege of Romans 8:29, that we might be "conformed to the image of his Son." It was by the crisis of suffering the Cross that he purchased our salvation. To a great extent, it is by suffering through crises in our lives that we are brought to maturity.

When we see the purpose of crises, it is possible to see, under the tutelage of the Holy Spirit, how we might go on to know in experience the Cross and its power.

"Now no chastening for the present seemeth to be joyous, but grievous: nevertheless afterward it yieldeth the peaceable fruit of righteousness unto them which are exercised thereby" (Hebrews 12:11).

Each crisis, which reveals the foundations on which we are basing our identity and acceptance, is an opportunity to exchange the identity which is of the flesh, our self-reliance, for that which is based on Christ's acceptance of us.

THE PATH OF CRISES

After we look at the path that crises follow, we can see how identity and acceptance are inextricably woven together in the fabric of personhood. While each can be discussed separately, neither can stand alone. That which gains us acceptance will be an important determinant in fixing our identity. The way we see ourselves, or that which gives us meaning, has much to do with where or with whom we seek acceptance.

Exactly the same circumstances can be viewed as drastically different depending upon the person's identity. For example, two persons might be completely bereft of every earthly possession. One sees himself as broke, while the other sees himself as poor. The first sees it as a temporary condition while the latter sees it as describing his person—his identity.

I have used the metaphor of a path to describe the way crises work. It is taken for granted that a path leads somewhere or there would be no reason for its existence. A path that leads nowhere leads to frustration. Likewise, a series of crises with no apparent meaning or discernible outcome seem like futility. It is only with the end or destination in view, in prospect or retrospect, that any good can seem to come from a series of negative circumstances or crises.

Those who have gone before can help us understand how to negotiate difficult terrain ahead. History tells of those who have suffered great privation, even loss of life, trying to gain material, psychological, or spiritual benefits. All the battles which are fought, within or without, are to gain or preserve something. Those who have found God's purpose in crises can act as spiritual guides for those who follow. Understanding the purpose of privation and suffering gives meaning and direction to the struggler, even though it may not lessen or shorten his suffering. For example, Moses "chose rather to suffer affliction with the people of God, than to enjoy the pleasures of sin for a season" (Hebrews 11:25). "Others were tortured, not accepting deliverance; that they might obtain a better resurrection" (Hebrews 11:35).

The Lord Jesus experienced great agony, both in Gethsemane and in his actual experience on the Cross. But he knew its purpose and its outcome. Therefore he was willing to pay the price. In like manner, those believers who would experience the freedom and joy of resurrection life must endure the privations and loneliness which lead to an experiential understanding of the Cross.

It is this path that I call the path of crises or the path to the Cross. To do so, the path is to be viewed as tandem crises in identity and acceptance, as two rails which compose a railroad track. The downward track and the upward track are depicted in the diagram which follows.

The diagram begins with the believer's new birth, at

CRISES AND IDENTITY

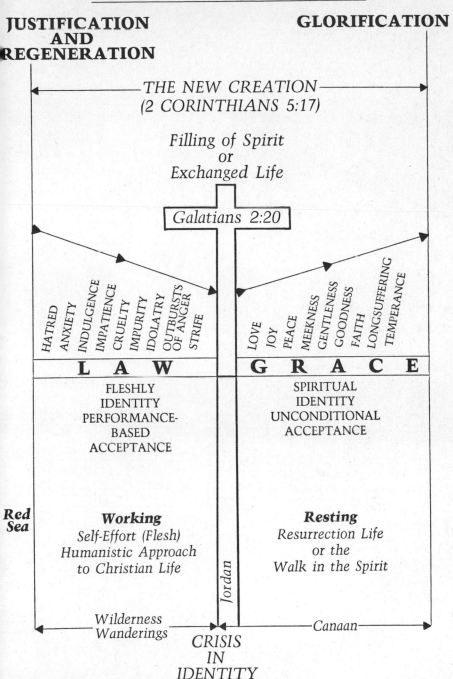

JUSTIFICATION AND REGENERATION

GLORIFICATION

THE NEW CREATION
(2 CORINTHIANS 5:17)

Filling of Spirit
or
Exchanged Life

Galatians 2:20

HATRED
ANXIETY
INDULGENCE
IMPATIENCE
CRUELTY
IMPURITY
IDOLATRY
OUTBURSTS OF ANGER
STRIFE

LOVE
JOY
PEACE
MEEKNESS
GENTLENESS
GOODNESS
FAITH
LONGSUFFERING
TEMPERANCE

L A W   G R A C E

FLESHLY
IDENTITY
PERFORMANCE-
BASED
ACCEPTANCE

SPIRITUAL
IDENTITY
UNCONDITIONAL
ACCEPTANCE

Red Sea

Working
*Self-Effort (Flesh)
Humanistic Approach
to Christian Life*

Resting
*Resurrection Life
or the
Walk in the Spirit*

Jordan

Wilderness
Wanderings

Canaan

CRISIS
IN
IDENTITY

which time he is *justified* and *regenerated*. Figuratively, this corresponds to the *Red Sea* experience and eventuates in the *wilderness wandering.*

Many through the years have used the history of Israel as an analogy of how God works in the life of a believer to bring him to the place of spiritual maturity. As Israel came out of the captivity of Egypt by crossing the Red Sea, so the believer leaves the captivity of Satan and sin by the regeneration experience. As Israel wandered through the desert for forty years because of their failure to depend on God, so the believer may wander and struggle for years in self-effort and never enter into the fullness of God's blessing and power. As Israel finally accepted God's lordship and entered into his power and protection by crossing the Jordan River into Canaan and to great victories that followed, so the believer comes to the place of complete surrender and enters into the life of blessing and power in a spiritual Canaan experience.

The wilderness wandering is largely a self-effort experience, a more or less humanistic approach to the Christian life. The path is basically downward, as man comes to the end of himself and human resources where the power of the crisis of the Cross is discovered.

Notice the path downward and how the rail of *identity* and the rail of *acceptance* have several crossties which bind them together and which keep in bondage all who would travel that way. The believer on this course has yet to understand experientially the truth of Galatians 5:1: "Stand fast therefore in the liberty wherewith Christ hath made us free, and be not entangled again with the yoke of bondage." In Galatians 2:19 we read, "For I through the law am dead to the law, that I might live unto God." But if we stop there without going on to Galatians 2:20, it is possible to live as though we were still under law while being dead to it.

The only way out of this dead-end course is up. The

problem is that we can't lift ourselves out of the dilemma. The crisis of identity is resolved when the Holy Spirit reveals to us the way out of the quagmire of self.

Notice how the track begins. At this point the traveler may be ignorant of the high road of freedom and resurrection life (grace) so he continues down the low road of bondage, basing his life on self-effort and acceptance based on performance, which is what we termed earlier, the *law*.

As the new believer, all fired up by his new birth, is ready to get under way on his spiritual journey, sometimes an old, cold saint has some cold water to dash his hopes and put out the fire of enthusiasm. Or he may be given an erroneous view of how to achieve true holiness. Without solid discipleship training, he is left with all the flippant challenges to "go for God," that he is "saved to serve," that he is to "walk the walk, to talk the talk, to move with the movers, to go with the goers, to make positive confessions, to love the lost, to judge the saved, to sink or swim," until he is dizzy from the exertion of self-effort and getting nowhere spiritually.

All too frequently, his home life suffers because he thinks he must remain on a treadmill of activity to stay "spiritual." The hyperactivity often obscures the problem and leaves little time for honest spiritual inventory. And, at times, a neurotic sinner becomes a neurotic saint and stays that way, or becomes worse, with the passing of time. Not only does time pass but responsibility grows and the increased demand may be met head-on with a diminishing supply of resources—his and others'.

When identity is based on accomplishments, the person must keep doing things, for failure to accomplish would result in what he sees as deficiency of being. Also, the accomplishments earn the praise of others and make the doer feel good about himself. The acceptance that is gained through the newly-earned identity provides double impetus toward new things to do.

At times the pursuits are secular and at times spiritual. Since both identity and acceptance are gained chiefly by self-effort, the proper response by the people who are significant in the seeker's life is the fuel which keeps him going.

As the traveler gathers momentum, as a train gathers speed, the rather insecure crossties cause the person to be built up for a letdown. No matter how well meaning we are, the best human effort can do nothing to hold the rails of acceptance and identity together; the frailties of the flesh, such as *hatred, anxiety, strife, impatience, cruelty, impurity, idolatry, outbursts of anger,* and *self-indulgence* come to the surface, making spiritual derailment imminent.

In our efforts to make ourselves look good, our *hatred* of those people who get in our way comes to the surface. We are filled with *anxiety, strife,* and *impatience* as we deal with those obstacles. Putting ourselves first, we become *cruel* and *impure,* we covet material things like *idolaters.* We have no *tolerance* for others, yet we *indulge* ourselves. That is the path our self-effort at achieving identity and acceptance naturally takes.

Some would attempt to replace the crossties with human counterfeits of the spiritual ones, as seen on the *grace* road. They look similar, but notice the difference: human love, happiness, tranquility, tolerance, kindness, human goodness, faith in faith, controlled temper, and rigid self-control. On the surface these appear to be better than the ones they replace, but both are the result of self-effort. Though the person might ask God consistently to help him to achieve these, they are still performance-based acceptance goals and designed to achieve identity based on fleshly self-effort.

As increasing amounts of self-effort are required to keep the tracks of identity and acceptance in place, one crisis after another is likely to be encountered.

When a married believer is traveling the fleshly road, he and his wife are both seeking their own separate goals, depending on their own effort. So long as they are proceeding toward mutual objectives, their paths are mistaken as being mutual and everything seems to be in harmony. Yet, both are finding identity and acceptance in different ends. One may be enjoying each mile of the journey while the other is consumed only with attaining the goal at whatever cost.

The children of such a marriage may adopt the goals of one parent or the other for a while, but eventually they must find their own direction. As the children begin to travel on their own journey through life, those goals which gave their parents meaning will not always suffice and they must find their own way.

Some people bring such great deficiencies into their marriage relationship that every day brings intrapersonal crises. When neither person is steady the intrapersonal crisis is very likely to cause interpersonal crises. The children may be caught in between or forced to go one way or another or to forge ahead on their own to reduce the conflicts.

In such crises none of those involved realize that the self-efforts of all combined will not be sufficient to eliminate the conflict within and between. It should be obvious by now that divergent paths must result in putting the relationships in tension. As each goes his own way, crises develop in each life with each impacting the other.

A common way of meeting the crisis is to readjust expectations from ourselves and others, set new secular and spiritual goals, ask God's help and direction, and dig in and work harder. Such efforts may dampen the crises time after time, but eventually a crisis which requires God's direct intervention will come up. No amount of self-effort nor strict adherence to God's standards of behavior, nor purchased help from counselors will suffice.

All self-effort in our analogy comes under the heading of *law* or *legalism*. True, the believer may insist that he is operating under *grace*, but his behavior may not bear it out. So long as he endeavors to fulfill God's revealed will by obeying scriptural principles without the power that comes from experiencing the Cross, he will be living after the flesh in a modified form of humanism.

When things begin to go awry to such an extent that outside help is required, the flesh tends to fleshly answers which do not include the Cross experience. Therefore, a variety of world-system developments with religious trappings are frequently employed to avert the inevitable—the crisis of the Cross.

All previous crises have taken the believer on a downward path to the final crisis so that the believer finds identity and acceptance in identification with Christ on the cross.

THE POWER OF CRISES

Someone said that man's extremity is God's opportunity. So long as there is any way out, no one would want to suffer the agony of a literal crucifixion. To a lesser degree, the Cross experience is equally abhorrent to the flesh. It is for this reason that some people will do everything in their power to make the flesh presentable just as it is, often trying to teach the flesh to serve God. To make it observe scriptural principles, they will dedicate it and rededicate it to the Lord. They will even commission it into full-time Christian service. But they shrink away from the Cross experience.

When the final crisis comes and with it the loss of self-esteem, the Cross becomes very appealing. Death is usually the last thing we want to think about when we are healthy and all is going well. But when the pain is no longer bearable, death can be a blessed release from suffering. Many who are terminally ill pray for the release death affords them.

After a crisis which has no human answer, the flesh is finally ready to capitulate. When every other avenue has led to a dead end, the death which took place at the time of the new birth from God's viewpoint becomes a revealed reality in the believer's experience. Paul described this death: "Knowing this, that our old man is crucified with him . . ." (Romans 6:6). Not only did Christ's death become ours but also his life—resurrection life—became a reality at one and the same time. Paul wrote: "For the preaching of the cross is to them that perish foolishness; but unto us which are saved it is the power of God" (1 Corinthians 1:18).

There may be a period of death throes at the time of a physical death, but when the end comes, the person simply lets go. Similarly, there may be many delaying tactics when it becomes clear that our co-death and co-resurrection with Christ are going to provide the only complete answer. But when there is no strength left in the flesh to struggle against the Spirit, it is the simplest thing in the world to let go of the self-life and exchange it for the life that lives in the union with Christ that Paul promised; "I am crucified with Christ: nevertheless I live; yet not I, but Christ liveth in me; and the life which I now live in the flesh I live by the faith of the Son of God, who loved me, and gave himself for me" (Galatians 2:20). Then the freedom from bondage and the peace that only the Spirit can give make us wonder why we resisted so long the Spirit who was urging us to walk with Christ.

For some people this experience of entering into the Spirit life is so radical and life-changing that it has been called by some groups, incorrectly, I believe, a "second work of grace," or "a baptism of the Spirit." Even though the changes are dramatic and life-changing, they result not from a second form of salvation but simply from the believer's entering into, or accepting in fact, what was already his by spiritual birthright.

Returning to the analogy of Israel, as God intended to lead his people directly from Egypt into Canaan, so he intended to lead the believer directly from regeneration into a walk in the Spirit. But as Israel sinned and ended up walking through the wilderness in self-effort, so many believers after salvation attempt to live the Christian life in their own effort and strength. They struggle in more defeat than victory until they choose to enter the "grace" way.

The Cross was not only a place of suffering. The Cross experience is also a place to end suffering. However, it doesn't end in death or the tomb but results in resurrection life.

Absolutely nothing changes regarding our standing before God when we enter into the Cross experience. Nothing is crucified at that time, for in God's reckoning we were crucified already with Christ. The moment we received Christ into our lives at salvation, we became partakers of his eternal life, and at that time we participated in his death, resurrection, ascension, and his being seated in the heavenlies (Ephesians 2:6). Though our participation in Christ's death and resurrection has nothing to do with our atoning for our sins, a person with a contrary theological position might erroneously interpret it that way.

The knowledge that he died for our sins and that he rose from the dead is sufficient basis for God's cleansing us from our sins. However, it is the knowledge that we died to sin that gives us victory over its power. These two events do not necessarily take place at the same time in experience or condition (state), though they do in position (standing).

The death and resurrection of the Lord Jesus Christ at Calvary was the turning point in history. The spiritual understanding of our co-death and co-resurrection with him will bring about just as great a turning point in our personal history as believers.

THE PRODUCT OF CRISES

Entering into the knowledge of the exchanged life on the basis of the experienced Cross is to the life of the believer what the Jordan River was to the children of Israel. They were delivered from the crises of their wilderness wanderings into an entirely new set of crises in Canaan. Some of the crises were more threatening than those experienced in the wilderness. There were undoubtedly those of the tribe of Israel who thought that they could rest on their laurels and do nothing, who thought God would do everything, who thought God should help them, or who thought they could help God.

When they were obedient to God and walked with him, it was he who pulled down the walls of Jericho. They did exactly as he commanded and he supplied the power. It is just so in the life of the believer today. After we have gone through the issue of surrendering our will and start living on the basis of our union with Christ in death and resurrection, it is still our responsibility to obey the clear injunctions of Scripture. It is his part to supply the power.

Returning to our diagram, we see the same two tracks of acceptance and identity as before, but there are some significant differences. The previous tracks were related to self-effort and progressed downward to the end of self and culminated in experiential understanding of our identification with Christ in his death and resurrection, the negative aspects of sanctification.

The Cross is also the beginning point for the positive

aspects of sanctification. Sometimes the process begins with a sudden realization of the truth but often the truth dawns gradually. The wilderness wandering, so to speak, may be only a few moments or days. It could, however, take a lifetime for some believers to stop trying to live the Christian life in their own strength and begin to trust Christ's life to be lived out in them by the Holy Spirit. The Spirit-filled believer still must find identity and acceptance and direction for life. The tracks leading upward from the Cross relate to God and direct the believer toward being conformed to the image of Christ. The terminal point is glorification, which comes at physical death, when the believer enters God's sinless presence. Then the believer is delivered from even the presence of sin.

When the Cross is understood by revelation of the Spirit, the believer realizes he is grounded in the Rock of Ages and finds his identity and acceptance in Christ. There is no cause nor possibility of being rejected by God, so the tracks are now firmly bound by what this union with Christ produces—the fruit of the Spirit— love, joy, peace, gentleness, goodness, faith, meekness, temperance, and self-control. As self-effort produced hatred, anxiety, strife, and the other works of the flesh, now the Holy Spirit living within supplies the power for a life of holiness and victory.

When the nation of Israel moved across the Jordan into Canaan, God promised them victory as long as they continued in trust and obedience. But this promise of God did not mean the Israelites would always obey him and find victory. In the same way we may not always be victorious. All of the ingredients for life and continuous victory are available to us, but so is the sin that yet dwells within us to deceive and detract from that which the Spirit would do in us and through us. Though the *old man,* that spiritual nature which we inherited from Adam, is crucified, and we reckoned ourselves dead to sin at identification, it is still possible for us to yield to sin and walk after the flesh (Romans 6:11; 7:17; 8:12). By walking after the flesh, I mean the return to self-effort rather than relying on the Spirit's work in us . . . "both to will and to do of his good pleasure" (Philippians 2:13).

When we return to self-effort, we revert to the tracks of our own making and seek again to establish a righteousness of our own rather than to submit in self-surrender to claim the power and the righteousness of God. Though the upward road is the way of *grace*, the believer may resort to former behavior patterns and live as though he were still under *law*. "Christ is become of no effect unto you, whosoever of you are justified by the law; ye are fallen from grace" (Galatians 5:4). Paul was not talking here of losing salvation, but of losing our power through living by self-effort and trying to keep scriptural commands without being ". . . delivered unto death for Jesus' sake, that the life also of Jesus might be made manifest in our mortal flesh" (2 Corinthians 4:11).

The believer who enters the high road of sanctification usually enjoys a respite of freedom and victory for varying lengths of time. The victory may be so sweet that he tends to stand and revel in the victory rather than to continue the walk in the Spirit. When such is the case he makes himself vulnerable to the "fiery darts of the wicked" (Ephesians 6:16). As the spiritual warfare begins, a new type of crisis is initiated for which most believers are not fully prepared. Entering into the life of grace promotes them to the front lines, but they need more basic training to prepare them for the hand-to-hand combat.

Not only is the flesh, or self-sufficiency, to be dealt with daily (Luke 9:23) and continually (2 Corinthians 4:11) but also the believer has two other enemies: the world and the devil. The deceitfulness of the flesh, the pull of the world, and the wiles of the devil combine together to force the believer to flee again and again to his only safe refuge, the Cross.

It is in Christ that we find an impeccable and immutable identity that allows us to face an uncertain world from the certain perspective of eternal values and goals. We can face the crisis of loss "as having nothing" and the temptation of the lost for worldly goods as "possessing all things" (2 Corinthians 6:10). It is, likewise, in Christ that we have an acceptance and a righteousness that is independent of human relationships. When we know that our identity and acceptance are immutable and anchored in realities that transcend this transient world, we can continue our journey undismayed by the inevitable crises.

Though crises may have an effect on our circumstances, they have no effect on our being (acceptance and identity) so long as we abide where we have been placed, where "our life is hid with Christ in God" (Colossians 3:3).

Crises will come and go, but the life of Christ remains unchanged, yesterday, today, and forever. The believer who abides in him will have a sure refuge and can stand as an island of security in a sea of dismay.

"Behold, what manner of love [unconditional acceptance] the Father hath bestowed upon us, that we should be called the sons of God [immutable identity]: therefore the world knoweth us not, because it knew him not" (1 John 3:1).

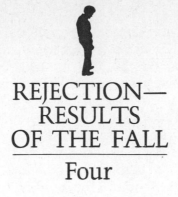

REJECTION—
RESULTS
OF THE FALL
Four

To find the genesis of rejection, we go back to the beginning, to Genesis, and see that the roots of rejection harken back to the roots of humanity—the first man. Adam was representative of all mankind as the federal head of the race. In fact, the rejection syndrome antedates Adam in that it started with Lucifer in his rebellion against God's authority. When Lucifer said, "I will . . . ascend into heaven, I will exalt my throne . . . I will sit also upon the mount of the congregation . . . I will ascend above the heights of the clouds, I will be like the most high," the sin of rebellion entered the universe (Isaiah 14:12-14).

As Lucifer rejected God's authority and tried to usurp it for himself, he was ejected from heaven with a host of angels and became the "prince of the power of the air, the spirit that now worketh in the children of disobedience" (Ephesians 2:2).

Satan appeared in the form of a serpent or "as an angel of light" (Genesis 3:1; 2 Corinthians 11:14). As he came on the scene, his first ploy was to cause Adam and Eve to doubt God's Word—an effective strategy which he continues to the present day. God had said they should not eat of that one tree in the garden or they would die. But Satan told Eve that, rather than dying, they would become as God. His deceit resulted in Adam and Eve's rebellion against God, just as Satan had rebelled.

Thus, Lucifer's rejection of God resulted in his causing rebellion and rejection in Adam and Eve, setting the rejection syndrome in motion. Satan's strategy was to try to undermine God's Word of promise to Adam and Eve, to convince them that God had rejected them by withholding from them. Satan accomplished his goal by half-truths. Adam and Eve didn't die at that moment in a physical sense. But the first couple died spiritually the moment they sinned; the "old man" of Romans 6:6 came into being immediately upon their spiritual death.

Eve's deception and Adam's deliberate transgression were the result of Satan's passing along his earned rejection to others. He told Adam and Eve they would not die and that they would become as gods (Genesis 3:5), another half-truth, and left them with the distinct impression that God had shortchanged them in denying them the knowledge of good and evil. The implication is that they were not made in God's image as Genesis 1:26 had stated, since they lacked such knowledge. Therefore, they could infer from the serpent's reasoning that God had lied to them or, to put it in terms of this discussion, that he had rejected them.

Based on this misinformation, they rejected God by rejecting his command and followed Satan's lead. As a fallen angel, Satan was ejected from heaven and they, in their fallen state, were ejected from the garden.

We can only speculate about Adam's spiritual nature immediately before and after the Fall. Was he a member of God's family and did he "die" out of it when he sinned? The Bible doesn't really say. We know only that Adam died spiritually on that day and that all of his descendents are "the children of the devil" unless they become, by the new birth, "the children of God" (1 John 3:10).

The rebellious nature of Adam and Eve, the "old man" of Romans 6, was passed along to their children, as evidenced in Cain, who rejected his brother Abel and slew him. From that time to this, our natural bent is to try to run our own lives and to fulfill our own needs in our own way, to our own advantage. The quest to meet our own needs apart from God is doomed to failure and frustration. The exploitation of others to get them to meet our needs—desires which can never be totally satisfied—results in more rejection. Since no human being can continually manifest perfect love, rejection is inevitable.

Just as Satan, in the form of the serpent, rejected Adam and Eve and was instrumental in their rejecting God, each of us since then has been rejected to some degree and, unless the process is halted, will pass that rejection on to children and others around us. The name of the game is: "Rejection, pass it on."

RESULTS OF REJECTION IN THE PERSONALITY

Every person since Adam is born separated from God— a living death. Thus separated from the source of life, man attempts to be his own source and resource and is doomed to a futile effort of trying to satisfy "the lust of the flesh, the lust of the eyes, and the pride of life" (1 John 2:16). The search frequently takes the form of inordinate sexual desires and perverted means of fulfilling them.

One such man was Virgil, married and with children, a blue-collar worker in his thirties. He was not a Christian and had frequently expressed his disdain for spiritual things.

He was diagnosed as a voyeur, involved in pedophilia

with young girls, and also expressed inordinately strong sexual drives, even with his wife. He had been arrested for his activities with young girls and had been under psychiatric treatment, but he found no help. He agreed to counseling, but told his wife he would walk out if religion were mentioned during the counseling session.

He had severe reading problems, possibly as a result of the extreme rejection he had received from his father. During the first interview, he accepted the Lord Jesus Christ and God began to do a significant work in his life. Three weeks later, he reported that the compulsions were gone. He could see women for the first time as something other than as sex objects. He had, for the first time in his life, a normal sexual drive toward his wife. His wife corroborated the drastic change in his life. Later a brother called and wanted to know what had happened to him. For the first time in their lives, the two of them were able to sit down and have a conversation together. Virgil had found an identity based on the Lord Jesus Christ rather than an insatiable drive for sexual thrills and fulfillment.

Before he rejected God, Adam had functioned as a truly integrated being. He was created as a three-part being with the spirit to rule over the personality or soul and the soul to rule over the body. His spirit was innocent, capable of fellowship with God in the spirit.

He had no hidden agenda of his own but was fully content to live in vital union with God and receive instruction and power for his day-to-day existence. When God told him to name all the animals, he had no inferiority complex to hamper his performance. He knew where he came from and who he was. He had no problem with identity, and his acceptance before God had never been called into question. Along with all other objects of God's creation, Adam had been pronounced by God as being ". . . very good."

People today try to find identity through identifying

with others, but Adam had no such problem. In the same way achieving could not earn him any more acceptance or acclaim because there were no onlookers except God until Eve appeared on the scene.

Since God is Spirit, Adam's vital relationship with God was spiritual. They enjoyed unbroken fellowship until such time as the union was broken by Adam's transgression. His sin set in motion a chain of events that resulted in his rejection of God's authority, bringing to all humanity alienation from God, alienation from others, and alienation within man himself.

ALIENATION FROM GOD

Whereas the soul was designed by God to function under the Holy Spirit's control through man's spirit, this was no longer possible due to the spiritual death which had taken place. Though Adam continued to function spiritually, he was not of his first father (God) by creation but of his second father (Satan) because of his sin.

All of Adam's descendants became alienated from God and stand in need of the reconciliation which has been provided in the Lord Jesus Christ.

ALIENATION FROM OTHERS

The person who suffers from the more extreme forms of rejection will inevitably alienate himself from others. The alienation may take some form of physical withdrawal, as becoming a loner, or it may be verbal withdrawal by becoming afraid to express deep feelings. It may also be emotional withdrawal, in indifference to or fear of close relationships. Alienation may take the form of "acting out" behaviors which serve to win others to oneself on the one hand or to fend them off on the other. The "acting out" may be friendly or hostile, depending upon the situation.

A person living his life in his own resources, and for himself, selfishly wants what he wants when he wants it. When more than one person is living selfishly, conflict is certain to arise. Since each is expressing his self life or flesh, selfishness will typify the life and life choices. As each is going his own way, doing his own things, their views, interests, and objectives will certainly clash.

The inborn and living-enhanced alienation is a natural inclination which rejects anything or anyone who dares to prevent its unhindered reign. People living close together will dispute boundaries—personal, social, political, and geographical. Wars between nations are but the extrapolation on a corporate level of selfishness within the individual.

The conflicts which ensue within the family will be passed on from generation to generation. The resulting personality traits, with the enslavement of the "old man" or old nature result in internal alienation as well.

ALIENATION FROM ONESELF

Alienation from oneself or rejection of oneself is a common phenomenon. Typically, most of our attitudes about ourselves are more learned than innate. We tend to value ourselves as others value us and we see ourselves as others see us—or, at least, as we perceive their evaluation and assessment of us.

Those who have been rejected by others are set up emotionally to reciprocate by displacing the rejection they feel onto those around them who may have no idea why they are being rejected. Those rejected from early childhood usually learn their lessons well and reject themselves in varying facets of their lives.

Such alienation or self-rejection may take the form of interpreting feelings of inferiority as fact rather than feeling. Putting oneself down, being critical of one's own accomplishments, and self-hatred are some of the indicators of self-rejection.

Those suffering alienation from themselves or self-rejection will foster such attitudes in their children. It is easy to see why the sins of the fathers can be passed on to the children and to the third and fourth generations.

Apart from a full understanding and appropriation of the grace of God in redemption, the alienation which is common to man will drive him to seek substitute answers. In many cultures it takes the form of attempting to appease evil spirits or some false deity. Each culture has some religious exercise through which its members attempt to bridge the gulf of alienation.

Alienation from God, others, and ourselves can only be bridged through the finished work of Calvary—redemption, reconciliation, and acceptance found in Christ.

ACCEPTED
IN THE BELOVED
Five

It is always good to get the good news before the bad. The good news is that what we are in Adam by our first birth can be nullified by rebirth into the life of the Lord Jesus Christ. We cannot help what we are by birth. That was thrust upon us. But we do have a choice about what we may become. "Wherefore, as by one man [Adam] sin entered into the world, and death by sin, and so death passed upon all men, for that all have sinned" (Romans 5:12).

Because we were born sinners, alienated and separated from God, we have a nature that leads us to commit sins. Again Paul wrote: "For all have sinned and come short of the glory of God" (Romans 3:23). Born as sinners, separated from God, we subsequently sin ourselves and bring upon ourselves the judgment of sin which Paul wrote about: "For the wages of sin is death; but the gift of God is eternal life through Jesus Christ our Lord" (Romans 6:23).

Born separated from God, we will remain separated from him eternally unless we accept his provision for being reconciled to him. The way of reconciliation is clear. Paul explained: "That if thou shalt confess with thy mouth the Lord Jesus, and shalt believe in thine heart that God hath raised him from the dead, thou shalt be saved. For with the heart man believeth unto righteousness; and with the mouth confession is made unto salvation. . . . For whosoever shall call upon the name of the Lord shall be saved" (Romans 10:9, 10, 13).

God has made the only provision needed for us to be reconciled to him and to be reconciled to others. Only he can forever deal with the alienation because of our being in Adam's race and because of our own sins. God asks only that we accept the truth that we are sinners, that we believe that he sent his Son, the Lord Jesus Christ to die for our sins, that we believe that he was buried and that he rose from the dead. He asks that we surrender our lives and turn from sin and trust Christ to forgive our sins. Anyone who is a child of God need never again feel alienated from him. However, we may have accepted Christ without having accepted our acceptance in him. One has to do with God's work of grace in us; the other has to do with our understanding and appropriating what has happened on our behalf.

It means the difference between heaven and hell to know that we have accepted Christ as our Savior and Lord. It can mean the difference between heaven and hell on earth as believers to know that he has accepted us. Our acceptance is based on nothing more or less than our being placed into, or baptized into, Christ by an act of the Holy Spirit in response to our act of faith.

Paul asked the Roman Christians: "Know ye not, that so many of us as were baptized into Jesus Christ . . . " Again he wrote: "For ye are dead, and your life is hid with Christ in God" (Colossians 3:3).

Our salvation and acceptance by God, being one and the same, is all of his doing and none of ours; "For by grace are ye saved through faith; and that not of yourselves: it is the gift of God: Not of works, lest any man should boast. For we are his workmanship, created in

Christ Jesus unto good works, which God hath before ordained that we should walk in them" (Ephesians 2:8-10).

Since we have God's immutable Word that we are his workmanship, we must not criticize or demean his creation by demeaning or rejecting ourselves. Many believers do not fully understand the basis of their acceptance, so they look to circumstances, to people, and to things, or to themselves, rather than "looking unto Jesus, the author and finisher of our faith" (Hebrews 12:2).

God has made us acceptable by making us righteous: "For he hath made him to be sin for us, who knew no sin; that we might be made the righteousness of God in him" (2 Corinthians 5:21). "And be found in him, not having mine own righteousness, which is of the law, but that which is through the faith of Christ, the righteousness which is of God by faith" (Philippians 3:9). Since God has declared us righteous, we must agree with him by faith and let him, by his Spirit, make true in us what he has said is already true of us.

Although we can claim immediately our acceptance in Christ or the filling of the Spirit by faith, the harmful effects of the rejection syndrome in the personality, particularly in the emotions, usually will not be immediately reversed. Feelings of a lifetime change slowly but change will definitely come in direct correspondence to our determination to appropriate the renewing of our minds by the Holy Spirit. What we know to be true, or what we think to be true, can have a direct impact on the way we feel—both emotionally and physiologically. For example, imagine a person who might be driving down a superhighway at eighty-five miles per hour. Classical music is playing on the radio, and the driver seems not to have a care in the world. Suddenly a car appears out of nowhere with lights flashing and siren blaring. The knowledge that he may be facing a trip to court, a big fine, and points on his driver's license may all flash through the driver's mind in an instant of time. There may be queasy feelings in the stomach as well. Then, as the patrol car pulls closer and the person is ready to pull over and face the consequences, suddenly the patrol car pulls around and goes on to answer a more urgent call. Now a new set of emotions begins to appear, based on new knowledge received in the mind. What was thought to be true, that he was going to be ticketed for speeding, resulted in fear and the emotions were upset and caused a corresponding physiological impact, the queasy stomach. As the situation was reversed, the new knowledge resulted in a change in the feelings, psychologically and physically, but a certain amount of time must pass before the process takes place and the person fully recovers.

What we believe is true about our condition can very definitely affect the way we feel. As the information comes that changes our beliefs, so will our feelings change. A person who has suffered emotionally from years of rejection can have better feelings about himself once he realizes his acceptance in Christ. But a lifetime of emotional patterns may not reverse themselves without some time lapse and without constantly reminding oneself that the old information—that he was unloved and rejected—is no longer true.

Once a person appropriates Christ as his life, the Holy Spirit will begin the process of renewing his mind, which will, in time, change the feelings of a lifetime, whether suddenly or gradually. "And ye shall know the truth, and the truth shall make you free" (John 8:32). The truth of God's Word, known in our minds and appropriated by faith, will be applied by the Holy Spirit to make freedom an experiential reality.

Should we not accept our acceptance in Christ, we can go on as believers being hounded by the rejection we have experienced and, by doing so, experience further rejection. At the same time, we can be desperately looking for acceptance in the same old places. If so, we can expect to see a continuation of interpersonal rejection, intrapersonal rejection, and a confused and confusing identity—one that may be based on behavior, one that will never satisfy, and one which continues to bring trauma to us and to others, as it did in the past.

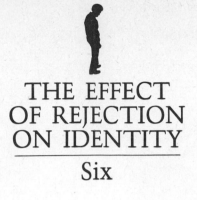

THE EFFECT
OF REJECTION
ON IDENTITY
Six

The people and things on which we base our identity and those from whom we experience acceptance are closely correlated. Identity may have to do with things, money, or power, but each of those must have people connected with them to be satisfying to any degree. A billionaire on an island by himself with all of the creature comforts possible would soon lose interest in such an affluent life. If there were no one to see what he has, to praise him for what he does, or over whom he could wield power, he would soon be able to assess accurately the true meaning of material things.

What we possess is meaningful only when compared to the possessions of others. What we do can be evaluated only in terms of similar efforts by others. Power which elevates us in our own thinking must be exercised toward other persons.

When identity is boiled down to its essence, it has always and only to do with other persons. All nonbelievers and most believers establish their identities based on their relationships with people—past and present.

Since a meaningful identity is the foundation for

acceptance, it is vital that we look at the crucial matter of identity. Upon what is it generally based and upon whom should it be based to stand the test of time and eternity?

AMNESIA: PSYCHOLOGICAL AND SPIRITUAL

Recently a lady who had suffered from amnesia for more than seven years was interviewed on national television. She had no clues as to her identity, nor could anyone be found who was acquainted with her. In a distant state, her mother saw her on television and immediately flew to the city where the woman was living and took her home. The woman's identity was reestablished by the mother who had borne her and by the family to which she had thus become related. Others with amnesia have remarried and had second families before finding out their true identity and learning that they had been previously married. When our identity is uncertain, it will cause problems with our meaning or purpose in life and will drastically affect our acceptance and resultant behavior.

The same kinds of problems exist in someone who does not know his true spiritual identity. Underlying the problems faced by many people who seek counsel is the core issue of identity. Often the real problem is not clearly understood at the beginning. Many believers do not suffer from spiritual amnesia, because the word "amnesia" suggests the person had known his identity but forgot it. Many believers have never known their true identity in Christ in the first place. Some have known and, seemingly, have forgotten. Others seem to know intellectually but have never had it revealed to them experientially by the Holy Spirit.

Christians often fall into the trap of basing their identity on people or the things of the world, just as their unsaved friends do. Their friends are lost for time and eternity, while the saved people are saved for eternity, but lost in time due to living with a false identity.

JESUS AND THE QUESTION OF IDENTITY
Jesus brought up the subject of identity to his disciples when he asked them, "Who do men say that I am?"

They replied, "John the Baptist, Elijah, Jeremiah, or one of the prophets."

Then Jesus asked a second and more penetrating question, "But who do you say that I am?"

Peter answered, "Thou art the Christ, the Son of the living God" (Matthew 16:13-16). Peter had properly identified the Lord Jesus, but subsequent statements and events revealed that he had not *identified with* the Lord Jesus. God the Father had revealed the true identity of the Lord Jesus to Peter so that he had correct intellectual information. He knew who the Lord Jesus was, but as yet he had no understanding of what Christ had come to do. As a result, Peter attempted to prevent the Lord Jesus from going to the Cross, rebuking Jesus when he told the disciples about his coming death. Peter was unwittingly identifying with the purpose of Satan to avert the victory of the Cross. Peter's identity and consequent behavior was of the flesh, not of the Spirit. He had understood the identity *of* Christ, but he had not understood his identity *in* Christ.

We need to ask ourselves these three questions: First, *who do men say, or who have men said, that we are?* Family, friends, teachers, employers, and others have communicated by verbal and nonverbal means, information on which we may have based our identity. Some of this information has been negative, and some has been positive. We may have been taught that we have worth, or that we are worthless. Our abilities may have been recognized and developed, or they may still lie dormant. We have received conflicting data from the various sources, with some having more importance attached to them than others. Out of all of this input from various sources over the years, believers as well as nonbelievers establish an identity based on this information or in reaction to it.

The second question is, *who do we say that we are?* Have we agreed with others that we are worthy or worthless or somewhere in between? Or have we set about to establish an identity of our own while denying the input we have received? In other words, have we passively accepted the prevailing opinion of people who are important to us, as to who we are, or actively denied it and built an identity based on achievements, power, or possessions? In either event the "others" have played a significant role in our identity.

Such identity is based on time and space relationships which have nothing to do with our true identity as believers. Yet our goals and daily pursuits will be a function of who we think or feel that we are when we are oblivious to our true identity in Christ.

The third, and most important, question is, *who does God say that we are?* Even as believers, God is not particularly impressed with our denominational labels nor our significant accomplishments—whether in or out of the church. Rank has no privilege in the church of the Lord Jesus Christ. Each member of the body must obtain, not attain, his or her meaning as a function of being baptized into Jesus Christ and his death and resurrection. However, many believers often attach much more significance to the Lord Jesus' becoming part of their lives than to their being united with his life. For that reason, such a believer will base his Christian identity on what he does for the Lord rather than who he is in the Lord. What the believer does should emanate from who he is. If he has spiritual amnesia, his identity will be based on works for the Lord rather than on the work of the Lord. Paul wrote that we are "created in Christ Jesus unto good works" (Ephesians 2:10). Such good works should be the normal, supernatural outgrowth of who we are in Christ. We should *be* in order to *do*—not *do* in order to *be*.

An identity based on works or achievements, even for the Lord, is a fleshly identity and will not stand the test of time, to say nothing of eternity. All identity that gives meaning is based on acceptance and vice versa. The struggle for acceptance may be keyed to the important "others" in our lives or it may be achievements which make it possible for us to accept ourselves. Others, however, must accept our achievements before the achievements have meaning to us. Therefore, it is really the opinions of others, not who God says we are, which are most influential in some people's lives.

What does God say that we are? And how does he see us presently as believers, regardless of our circumstances, psychological makeup, or behavior? To answer this question we must also know where he says we are, since it is where we are that establishes who we are. Paul wrote, "But of him are ye in Christ Jesus, who of God is made unto us wisdom, and righteousness, and sanctification, and redemption" (1 Corinthians 1:30). However, many who know Christ Jesus as their redemption never know him experientially as their wisdom, righteousness, and sanctification.

To know Christ in these dimensions means that we must know not only that he is in us but also that we are in him. We are in him, and he is seated at the right hand of the Father, where we also are, according to Ephesians 2:6. Since we are seated at the right hand of the Father, in the Lord Jesus we are obviously accepted, not on the basis of what we have done, but on the basis of what he has done, the finished work of Calvary.

In the book of Ephesians, Paul used the equivalent of "in Christ" more than one hundred times. The fact that we are in Christ eternally carries with it the truth that we are in Christ crucified, buried, ascended, and seated in heaven. We are identified with him and all that he is—including his righteousness.

Since our true identity derives from the One in whom we are, it must be appropriated by faith and cannot be achieved, enhanced, or delimited by works of any sort. It is based on his work for us at Calvary, not to any degree on our work for him after that.

We need to ask ourselves, "Do I know who I am? Have I lived my Christian life based upon a false identity where the opinions of others have been paramount—upon who men have said I am? Or, have I been saddled with an identity of my own making, upon who I say I am?"

If either of these is true of us, then we are suffering from spiritual amnesia and do not know, in experience, who God says we are. We must, by faith, declare to be true what God says is true, that we have been identified with him in death, burial, resurrection, ascension, and in being seated in the heavenlies. We must give up our life and everything upon which we have based our identity, however good or bad, in exchange for the Christ-life.

Upon our answer and our faith transaction depends our usefulness to the Lord Jesus. We will either abide in ourselves and reap the results of walking after the flesh, or we will abide in him and know the peace and joy of walking in the Spirit, fulfilling God's purpose for us in this life.

LIVING TO SUCCEED— IDENTITY THROUGH DOING

Seven

In the world, hard work and success go hand in hand. The natural mind, strongly motivated by pride, finds this idea appealing because it suggests that there is something the individual can do to merit the goal toward which it strives. The person operating from a carnal mind also sees spiritual victory or spiritual goals being achieved as the result of his own dedicated self-effort. God, rather than being the life source, is considered only someone to help him in his spiritual endeavors.

Many self-help and positive-thinking approaches to Christian living are taught in such a way that they are trying to aid the flesh in carrying out God's commands. In this scheme of things, Christian living becomes just a list of do's balanced by a list of don'ts, resulting in a life based on what can be called legalism.

As the name implies, legalism places the emphasis on keeping the law rather than on grace. Both in the individual's personal life and church life, God's commands are carried out by the legalist in whatever energy of self-effort can be produced, without being aware of how it is done. Spirituality or the quality of one's

Christianity is measured almost entirely on how well the do's and don'ts are observed.

In preaching and in personal work, a legalistic church teaches the believer clearly and scripturally that he is saved by grace through faith, but immediately the believer is put under the law and told to perform. Without the instruction as to how he may be empowered to perform or to keep these standards through the experienced Cross, the knowledge of the Spirit's indwelling power and controlling influence, the believer begins to experience not the acceptance he seeks but further rejection.

Christians and Christian churches that are fulfilling the Great Commission, in obedience to God's commands genuinely love the lost. The sinner is loved despite his despicable sins. Believers that have a burden for souls and love the *lost* sometimes have little love and patience with the *saved* who don't meet their expectations of what is right or wrong.

Only those who are able to knuckle down and keep the rules are considered to be "good Christians." In such a scheme, the fruit of the Spirit is often considered to be another soul led to Christ, rather than what the Holy Spirit would produce in us, as defined in Galatians 5:22, 23.

When the believer has dedicated and rededicated himself to the Lord until he reaches the desperation point, he may seek counseling to find the way of victory he hasn't been able, through self-effort, to find. The counseling he receives may tell him to substitute a scriptural behavior or thought pattern for an unscriptural one. A person working in the flesh could be taught to do so and may even seek the Holy Spirit's aid to strengthen his own self-efforts. The Bible used in such a fashion is unwittingly used as a manual for behavior modification. When legalistic teaching such as this has failed to provide victory, a counselor trained in the fine art of applied legalism may be employed to enhance the flesh to carry out the commands of the Scriptures.

Legalism has often been referred to as a form of Pharisaism, since it gives so much attention to the letter of the law but little to the spirit of the law. However, another parallel can be drawn which would fit some Christians, even those who are not necessarily legalistic in their approach to the Christian life.

The Pharisees had a firm belief in the God of the past, the God of Abraham, Isaac, and Jacob. They also believed in the God of the future, the resurrection of the dead, and the coming of the Messiah.

In like manner, Christians may be certain of their past experience with the Lord Jesus in salvation, and may have a firm anticipation of his return to earth. And yet they don't know the victory of the resurrection life as a present reality. As with the Pharisees of old, the past is settled, and the future certain, but the present is troublesome.

The Pharisees of old denied the incarnation of Jesus, God with them, whereas modern-day Pharisees deny the reality of the Son of God in them as they live day by day. The former were slaves to the law while the latter are slaves to the dictates of self and the flesh.

They are alike in denying the reality of Jesus in the present and his relevance to their present situation. The Pharisees of old were in the flesh while the modern-day versions walk after the flesh.

The self-help approach to Christianity has always been in vogue. At times it is the persistent application of legalism and at other times it is religious attention to self-improvement programs, individual and corporate.

Programs to enhance motivation and self-image are numerous and many are targeted toward Christian audiences. Promises of success in finances, public speaking, self-confidence, programmed goals, feminism, advancement in career, and many others lure Christians and others to expend great amounts of time and money to find satisfaction for the flesh. Tapes and booklets are sold by the thousands, torturous weekends are spent in a variety of sensitivity groups for self-exploration and self-expression—TA groups are even held in churches which run the gamut of Christianity and psychology.

Some people will use almost anything the world develops to enable them to meet their own needs. Scriptures sprinkled around through the materials change the flavor but not the essence of the materials such programs use. When the same basic approach presented in these programs will work as well for the non-Christian as for the Christian, it would seem obvious that the Holy Spirit is not the author nor the empowering agent of such materials.

On the corporate scene, churches are prone to the same methods of operation as that of their constituent members. Studies are made and programs are launched one after the other which may be patterned after secular programs with only slight adaptations. Recruiting for personnel to staff the programs may also be strangely reminiscent of the tactics used in the world.

When such programs are not led of the Holy Spirit, it should come as no surprise that they are not blessed with miraculous results. Though some positive results may be seen, it may be more due to positive thinking and soulish enthusiasm than to the direct intervention of the Holy Spirit. When the results can be predicted and explained, it is likely that the Spirit had little to do with it.

Programs can be spawned by the flesh, carried out by the flesh, and see mostly fleshly results. As in the individual so in the corporate body. It isn't long before the flesh tires of being cranked up. When fatigue sets in, a replacement program, frequently staffed by replacement personnel, is set in motion.

Whole churches go through the same cycle while the members, in their private and church lives, suffer defeat and desperately yearn for a life that they can not explain in terms of their own efforts.

The identity of the church is made up of that of its membership. The church, like its members, is *doing* in order to *be*, with the success or failure frequently assessed in terms of numbers, people, and money. As such, more attention is given to the breadth of the ministry than to its depth. When the church's vision is inward rather than upward, the self-centeredness will eventually be readily apparent to all within and without.

Unless self-effort is dealt with by the Cross, our behavior may rigidly be brought into agreement with Scripture passages dealing with *doing*. However, ignoring those passages dealing with the experienced Cross and the appropriation of victory by faith results in causing the life of *being* to go begging.

The believer's identity and acceptance in this system are based on *doing* in order to *be*. In the next chapter we will see that the scriptural order is that of *being* in order to *do*.

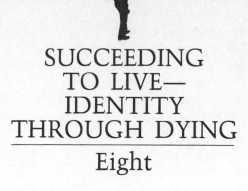

SUCCEEDING TO LIVE— IDENTITY THROUGH DYING
Eight

To most believers, it makes little sense to inform them that success comes out of failure, gain out of loss, victory through defeat, and life out of death. Many want the peace, joy, and power of resurrection life, but few desire the death of the Cross which is the precursor to that life. Crucifixion precedes resurrection life. The Cross was never popular and never will be. Self-effort is appealing and many Christians will work themselves to death to keep from dying! Others try so hard to die that they can't live.

As we are not to *work* in order to *be*, but to *be* in order to *work*, we understand what Paul was explaining: "We are created in Christ Jesus unto good works." Just as an emphasis on law at the expense of grace leads to legalism, so emphasis on grace at the expense of obedience leads to passivity and license.

One of the main criticisms leveled at the "deeper life" teaching, of the experienced Cross or exchanged life experience, is that its adherents tend to become passive about obedience. This criticism is sometimes justified, for some people do tend to swing from law to grace and not strike a balance between the grace and obedience taught by the Scriptures.

Though excesses are never justifiable, it is at least understandable that one who has never had freedom might tend to revel in its newness before he settles down to work *in* the Lord more effectively than he ever worked *for* the Lord.

Salvation is by grace through faith. Victory and acceptance are obtained the same way. Paul made this point to the Galatians: "Are ye so foolish? Having begun in the Spirit, are ye now made perfect by the flesh?" (Galatians 3:3). The answer was obviously no. That which began as a spiritual work must continue as a spiritual work.

Our righteousness, which makes possible our acceptance, is appropriated by faith, and our victory is also a gift to be received by faith. Such faith is our acceptance and trust in the finished work of Calvary, not only the blood of Christ which dealt with what we have done, but the Cross of Christ which deals with what we are by nature, born as we were into the world as sinners.

Victory, acceptance, and identity, in the eyes of unbelievers and carnal believers, is sought through doing, whereas the Bible teaches that they are obtained through dying. While the Lord Jesus was yet on earth prior to his crucifixion, he was tempted by Satan. After the resurrection, sin had no more power to tempt him because he had died to it (Romans 6:10). Likewise, he was victorious over Satan who had been put under his feet.

In the same way we are to count ourselves as having died to sin, "for he that is dead is freed from sin" (Romans 6:7). In other words, our victory was won back at the Cross in our death to sin—not in our struggle to overcome it, but because we are in Christ, the Victor who was and is victorious over sin.

But how can we be dead to sin and still respond to it? Did we die and are we now dead to sin? Intellectual understanding of our experiential victory must be based on a scriptural model of man. Only as God allows us to see ourselves as he sees us—spirit, soul and body—can we logically understand how we can be dead to sin and yet commit sin, respond to it, or in any way be under its power.

We must understand our death if we are to know the reality of resurrection life. Only as we realize we died to who we were can we revel in the knowledge of what we are. Our identity and acceptance derive from the One we are in, not from the manner in which we perform. These truths are understood from the Word and accepted by faith.

Some of the misunderstanding about our relationship to the crucified and resurrected Christ arises from an incomplete understanding of man himself. As we seek to know who we are and the basis on which we can be justified and sanctified by faith, it may help us to see how others view the makeup of man. Seeing man as being of only two parts, that is, holding a dichotomous model of man, may lead to a form of righteousness and acceptance based on self-effort. The term *dichotomy* is used often in theological studies to discuss the makeup of man. The word is from two Latin words meaning "two" and "cut apart." According to this model, man has a body and a soul, a material part and an immaterial part.

The *trichotomous* view holds that man has three essential parts, body, soul, and spirit. The trichotomous view, or the three-part model of man, seems to be more supporting of the teaching that righteousness comes by faith. Acceptance based on our identity in Christ, jointly crucified, buried, raised, and seated in the heavenlies with him, upholds the doctrine of grace.

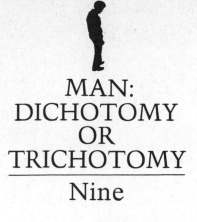

MAN:
DICHOTOMY
OR
TRICHOTOMY
Nine

The two more common models of man are the two-part view, called *dichotomy*, and the three-part view, called *trichotomy*. The dichotomous model holds that man has a material part, the body, and an immaterial part, the soul. Such a view is feasible in that the immaterial part may be defined in numerous ways. Some have defined the immaterial part of man as the mind, but most dichotomists call it the soul.

Those who accept the trichotomous model say that man consists of a spirit, soul, and body. Those of this view are, perhaps, in the minority today, as many Bible scholars believe that biblical language is not precise concerning the immaterial part of man, making it not possible or practical to theorize about man's immaterial nature.

Because most Christians see no practical relevance in holding to strong conclusions about their immaterial makeup, the discussion of dichotomy and trichotomy is viewed as theological hairsplitting. But if Christians can be shown that a clear understanding of the soul's relationship to the spirit of man can clarify and solve practical problems that face him every day, the distinction may be worth understanding.

Both those who adhere to trichotomy and to dichotomy can be faulted for their lack of concise definition of consistent terms. Because we have seen the strong interdependency of identity and acceptance in man, we need to examine both models of man to see which better accommodates an explanation of the cause and solution to these needs and which of the two is more consistent with biblical language. In doing so, we are not dealing with mere theological abstractions.

Since man is essentially a spiritual being, even though he has a physical body, his identity must have to do with God, the ultimate spiritual Being to whom he relates. Such identity must be based not upon what man has done but upon what the Lord Jesus Christ has done for him if we are to accept what the Scriptures teach about this relationship. Since man is spirit and he has a soul, the attributes of the soul should reflect who he is in the spirit. When he is joined to the Lord, he finds acceptance, and when he is one spirit with the Lord, he has found immutable identity. "But he that is joined to the Lord is one spirit," Paul wrote (1 Corinthians 6:17).

Theologians past and present have grappled with the task of describing the makeup of man. Scholars produced by a host of sectarian biases are divided or polarized on the issue. Some take 1 Thessalonians 5:23 literally and hold the view that man has a spirit as well as a soul (personality) and body, which has been labeled the trichotomous view. Others, equally well schooled and firm in their belief that the Bible is the Word of God, staunchly contend that man does not have a spirit as a separate *entity* (though they may refer to the spirit as a facet of the soul) but, rather, is comprised of soul and body, the dichotomous position.

What can we profit by laying side by side the dichotomous and trichotomous models of man to make contrasts and comparisons? Finding a scriptural model of man will aid the believer in understanding his intrapersonal functioning and his standing before God. Also, the articulation of this liberating truth through teaching or counseling is greatly enhanced. A Christ-centered counseling theory or approach must be anchored and be congruent with a model of man which leads to a scriptural definition of the spiritual life as Paul stated it: "Not I but Christ . . ." (Galatians 2:20).

Many theological issues, such as the question of dichotomy or trichotomy, remain unsettled because theology is man's rational attempt to systematically organize the truths of the Bible. While we must accept the Bible as being absolute truth, man's ability to organize infinite wisdom is limited by his finite mind. So biblical theology, no matter how wise or spiritual the man who systematizes it, should never be put on a parity with the Scriptures. Such studies are helpful, but not infallible.

Perhaps the strongest biblical evidence for a three-part model for man is found in Paul's words: "I pray God your whole spirit and soul and body be preserved blameless unto the coming of our Lord Jesus Christ" (1 Thessalonians 5:23). The way these three Greek nouns were used sets them forth as three separate entities. First, they were joined by *kai*, the main coordinating conjunction: spirit *and* soul *and* body. Also, each noun, *pneuma* (spirit), *psukee* (soul), and *soma* (body) were preceded by definite articles, strong grammatical evidence that the author was talking about three distinct things.

Such a three-part constitution of man might tempt some of us to try to make a parallel with man and the Trinity. Such an analogy fails because the Trinity is constituted of three Persons in One and man is but one person. The biblical language of Genesis is also important: "The Lord God formed man [body] of the dust of

101

the ground and breathed into his nostrils the breath of life [spirit—the word for "breathed" and "breath" can also be translated "spirited" and "spirit"] and man became a living soul [soul]" (Genesis 2:7).

The dichotomists say that man is capable of spiritual relationships, that he can function spiritually, though he has no spirit as a separate entity. Many of them argue that it makes no difference which position one takes about man's immaterial part so long as it is granted that it properly explains how man relates to God. In this case they are talking about function and not entity.

Certainly there are Spirit-filled people who walk in the Spirit and are greatly used of the Lord who deny that they have a spirit. However, this denial does not preclude the possibility that they have a functioning spirit which is being described by them as a spiritual function of the personality or soul. It is undoubtedly possible for an individual to walk in a truth of which he has little or no knowledge.

Often Christians are not concerned about their inner makeup because they haven't seen how it affects their lives. Such a tendency is sometimes a reaction to those who try to force certain Scriptures to fit a system and to analyze experience in the light of the system rather than allowing the Holy Spirit to speak directly through the Word.

This is not to be construed as an appeal to ignorance or any assault on the study of systematic theology. However, some excellent proponents of systematic theology are often unfruitful when it comes to living the concepts or in transferring such concepts in life-transforming ways to others.

Theology that produces no transformed lives, nor solves any human problems becomes an exercise in futility. The same can be said of Bible knowledge without the system, such knowledge without application to the life by the Holy Spirit may lead only to intellectual pride instead of spirituality.

Though it isn't absolutely necessary to have perfect intellectual understanding of some scriptural truths to appreciate the results by faith, it is difficult to convey such truth accurately to others while having a faulty understanding of it. For example, some people who walk in victory in Christ hold a dichotomous view of man, while others who walk in victory hold a trichotomous view of man. There are also those who walk in victory in Christ who do not know the difference. Thinking the distinction has no practical relevance, they haven't even taken the time to develop a working definition of the soul or the spirit of man, the functions of one or each—much less the interface between the two.

To point up the issue and expose the ignorance in psychological as well as spiritual circles, the preface of a recent psychology textbook stated that the psychologist does not work in the realm of the soul. If not, one might well ask, where then does he work?

Many pastors who would argue for a trichotomous view of man frequently confuse the terms in the pulpit, using them inappropriately. When we speak of the soul being "saved," as in 1 Peter 1:9, the hearer frequently infers that the primary work of regeneration occurs in the soul. It is clear that the spiritual rebirth is the subject under consideration, so it is the spirit which is made new. The word *psukee* in Greek is frequently translated "life" when it is clear from the context that the writer is using soul to refer to the whole person or the life principle.

Many of those holding a trichotomous position would agree that the spirit has been regenerated. Those holding a dichotomous view might say that soul or personality is reborn. Others of them might incorrectly use

Romans 8:11 as a proof text to assert that the body is reborn as well, though it is clear from Christ's words to Nicodemus that the new birth did not mean a physical rebirth. The redeemed will receive glorified bodies, but not until Christ returns and the saints, alive and resurrected, are glorified (1 Corinthians 15).

Is this a soulish or psychological rebirth that we are discussing? The way one answers this question hinges on the nature of Adam's death at the Fall. Did Adam die psychologically or spiritually, or did he die at all?

ADAM'S DEATH

Adam was commanded not to eat of the tree of the knowledge of good and evil, "for in the day that thou eatest thereof thou shalt surely die" (Genesis 2:17).

If we conclude that Adam died in some sense, we must determine what died that day. Since Adam continued to walk, think, talk, and make decisions, he obviously wasn't physically dead. Likewise, he could reason that he needed to fashion some kind of covering for himself, so his personality or soul continued to function in a logical manner, although in different directions.

A dichotomous view of man must allow for a spiritual function or facet within the personality, since in this view spirit doesn't exist as a separate entity. Therefore, this view seems to argue that what died in Adam was a function, which would seem a contradiction in terms. A function can cease but it doesn't seem reasonable to say a function "dies," or is separated from God, as some would define death. Some part of the personality had to die which would have left Adam a psychological cripple, a theory that would be difficult to support from Scripture.

God decreed Adam's death the very day he ate of the tree, and since God doesn't lie, some kind of death took place. Some would make Adam's death a *positional* death. If his death were positional only and not experiential, it would seem that Adam could relate to either God or Satan until his actual physical death took place. Also, such a positional death could be considered spiritual in nature or it could encompass soul and body as well. It would then have to be determined whether man after the Fall was really depraved in practice or only in position. If the spirit (or whatever died), in actuality, were no more dead than the body, it would continue to function much the same as before. Likewise, the soul or personality would be contaminated by sin only positionally, but not actually.

Judicially, man would be dead, or have death and separation from God imputed to him, but practically speaking, he could still relate to God, even though he had deliberately transgressed in responding to Satan. Seemingly, he would have the best of both worlds.

If this were true, Adam would only seem to be dead to God, positionally, and alive to Satan in the same way, positionally. Jeremiah wrote: "The heart is deceitful above all things, and desperately wicked: who can know it?" (Jeremiah 17:9). If Adam died positionally only, then he and his progeny were positionally related to Satan. Then the heart Jeremiah spoke of is only positionally and not actually deceitful. But Jeremiah's comment sounds very much as if man is fallen in experience as well as in position. Man after the Fall is either depraved or he isn't. He either died in the Garden of Eden or he didn't.

If Adam actually died that day, it must have been his spirit that died. If this is true, Adam either had no spirit after his death or he had an unregenerate spirit that could relate to Satan but no longer to God. Since Jesus could say that Satan was the father of certain people, some part of fallen man must be of the same essential nature as Satan for the kinship to be actual, not positional. When Paul was describing what Christ had done for us, he began by saying that something in us that was dead had been quickened, made alive (Ephesians 2:1-6). Paul also must have been talking about something that occurred in regard to man's spirit.

The presence of a spirit in fallen man makes it possible to have spiritual union and communion with Satan, the god of this world. Assuming the presence of a spirit, Adam died a spiritual death and could no longer relate to God. However, he became intimately related to Satan.

This corrupt spirit, which I believe is identified in Romans 6:6 as the "old man," is Satan's agent in fallen or natural man to enslave him to sin. Were it only the power of sin in the soul, man would have the choice to yield and obey sin or refuse to yield and be righteous. Slavery indicates ownership or possession. A choice did not remove a slave from the ownership of his master. Redemption through purchase was the only method of changing owners.

When the sinner is redeemed from slavery to Satan, his basic nature is changed. The old man is crucified and "put off" while the new man that came into being through rebirth is "put on." A death and a birth take place; the crucifixion of the old man signals death out of Satan's family, and regeneration signals entry into God's family. The unbeliever, through the old man, is identified with Adam. The believer, through the new man, is identified with Christ.

While those who hold the dichotomous position agree that a new birth is necessary, the dichotomous model would more logically support a theory which would contend that man's essential nature could and should be improved. According to this view, the "old man" is viewed variously as an entity or all that we were in Adam, or a function of the personality. It would be as difficult, however, to explain the birth of a function as the death of one.

The Bible however, clearly teaches that Adam, as a result of the fall, experienced a death with spiritual ramifications, and became a child of Satan. He became a slave to sin, which was authored by Satan, and man became responsive to Satan rather than to God. Similarly, the believer has died a death and has had a simultaneous birth (Romans 6:6; Galatians 2:20; John 1:13; Titus 3:5; John 3:5, 6).

It is here that the dichotomous view must resort to a judicial or positional death because it allows for no part of man which can die without losing the man. Since the spirit is construed to be a function rather than an entity, the "old man" of Romans 6:6 can not literally be crucified as the Scripture states. To be consistent with this rationale, the dichotomous view must hold that there is no literal rebirth but a judicial or positional one that is imputed to the personality. However, most dichotomists would say that man has a literal rebirth but a positional crucifixion with Christ.

If we generalize from the dichotomist view, and allow that the person is born again, we yet have the problem of dealing with the power of sin, which didn't die. How will we instruct him so that he might live a victorious life? Again we encounter a problem similar to the one encountered before, of whether or not the Cross became a reality in a person's life. The dichotomous view contends that the old man is not the sin nature or the corrupt spirit, so it is inconsistent to say that it could be crucified or replaced by a regenerated spirit. Similarly, it would be impossible for the believer to reckon or count continuously upon his death to sin as the basis for freedom from sin's reign, if he contends that nothing in the believer is, or was, crucified.

If the believer is provided no means of effectively and

experientially dealing with the flesh, his only recourse is to walk after the flesh and attempt to obey scriptural injunctions, and ask God to help and strengthen him. The result is a life of strife and struggle for victory over the flesh, while walking after the flesh—an impossibility, according to Romans 7. Such a life must, by definition, be a life of *doing* instead of *dying*, since the model admits of no provision for the application of the Cross to the self-life or flesh.

On the other hand, if we allow that the old man is a spiritual entity which was put to the Cross of Christ, the believer also has a regenerate spirit (new man) which restricts the power of sin to the soul and the body. Not only can sin not touch the spirit nor defile it, but the spirit is also indwelt and empowered by the Holy Spirit. This means that the self-same power that God used in raising the Lord Jesus Christ from the dead is available within the spirit of the believer (Ephesians 1:19, 20; Romans 8:11). The sin nature (old man) having been crucified, the believer's will is the agency that swings the balance of power, by choosing the power which is to control the personality—either the power of indwelling sin or the power of the indwelling Holy Spirit, the ". . . law of the Spirit of life in Christ Jesus" or ". . . the law of sin and death" (Romans 8:2).

Satan, the enemy of souls, has made another critical deception in blinding the minds of believers to the truth that the old man or sin nature no longer exists in the Christian. Thus, he has influenced many believers into expending vital energy in fighting a supposed battle within their spirits between the old and new natures, a battle the Holy Spirit won quite decisively at the new birth. The Holy Spirit has established a permanent residence within the regenerated spirit of the believer. When sins in the believer's life are imputed to the old man or old nature, the flesh, a condition of the soul, which actually causes the sins in a believer, is merely provided a decoy which camouflages its operations. Whether or not a believer sins is a decision of the will of the believer; either he has yielded his members to sin or he has yielded himself to God. Victory is not attained but obtained, or appropriated, by counting oneself to be dead to sin and alive to God, as commanded by Romans 6:11. However, if a believer doesn't know he died to sin in Christ, he is rather unlikely to have confidence in a recurrent application of the Cross to the power of sin as the sole path of victory.

The believer's only other recourse would be to espouse a works orientation and try to live a life pleasing to God by self-effort. This, of course, is an attempt to strengthen the flesh for the inevitable battle with the Spirit (Galatians 5:17) which is the source of conflict within the Christian. If there were no part of man which could be rendered inoperative by the Cross, then the Cross would accomplish nothing for us in dealing with the power of sin.

CONCLUSION
The model of man as being spirit, soul, and body is to me absolutely essential in explaining man. Since the believer is not a sinner who is saved, but a saint who may still sin, God's assessment of man is that he *is* righteous, though he may *behave* unrighteously. For this to be something more than just a word game, there must be a part of man that is made righteous, not just reckoned or accounted to be so.

Since the Lord Jesus Christ paid the penalty for the guilty sinner, God can pardon him and still be just. God's justice has been satisfied so he will no longer judge the believer guilty for what he has done. However, being forgiven for transgression does not change in any way what man *is.*

Can the judge release a man who is still a criminal

reprobate and with no choice or capacity to stop his crime (sins)? Can God set a man free with no recourse but to continue in the same condition? Such an action might be legal but it would not be moral. Although human justice might do so, God could not. Could his holy nature permit him to justify a sinner and yet leave him a sinner by nature?

Not only has God done something for the sinner by payment for his sins by the blood of the Lord Jesus Christ, but also he has done something in him through the Cross of Christ. Scripture does not teach that something was merely added to man or accounted to him, but that man was regenerated and made a new creation.

THE CHURCH,
THE COLLEGE,
AND COUNSELING
Ten

Many believers today struggle in defeat, rejecting and being rejected, while our Bible schools and seminaries continue to pump into the mainstream men and women who desire to help believers in their struggles. Unfortunately, many of them have majored in how-to-do subjects instead of how-to-be instruction. Many of the students have the kind of spiritual life that has not kept pace with their theological knowledge. Many are well equipped to do evangelism but not as well equipped to disciple those so evangelized.

Part of the problem may be that some theological institutions lack a definition of the spiritual life which is consistently used in every department and course taught in the institution. Unless there is a single model of man coupled with a unifying definition of spiritual life consistent with that model, theological positions may not align well with policies and practices. One department may be teaching one view of man and another department contradicting that view.

A person called into the ministry must not only be able to define spiritual life but must also be walking in it if he is to lead others into spiritual living. When this is true, his life, his preaching, his teaching, and his counseling for discipleship will be so integrated that he will not have to change gears when he moves from one form of ministry to another.

A person prepared to help believers to understand the rejection on which they have based their identity and who can lead them to an understanding of who they are in Christ is a person who understands experientially the life that is in Christ.

Some, however, live a spiritual life but can't articulate it because they hold to a model of man and to terminology which cannot explain their experience in terms of the teaching of God's Word. These are often the ones who say that the distinctions between terms such as old man, flesh, and sin are largely semantic issues. As I discussed this with one minister who is being greatly used of God in the pastorate, he said, "I believe what you are talking about is just a question of semantics."

As the conversation continued, he openly admitted that the truths of Romans 6, even though a reality in his own life, were the most difficult to get across to his congregation of any truths in the Bible. To this I replied, "It's just semantics." Because the terms were not clear in his thinking, they were not clear in his teaching.

When there are uncertain or ambiguous definitions of theological positions and terms, the educational institution, in the interest of academic freedom, leaves the student to make his own choice. On other occasions there may not be sufficient confidence in the correctness of a particular theological position to stake the reputation of the institution upon it.

But churches, institutions, and schools should cease the subtle rejection of students by failing to give them a definite position on that about which God makes definite statements. It is by far the more popular position to take no position on some of these issues that we have found to be absolutely vital to a victorious walk in Christ. Some who hold to inerrancy of the Scriptures might contend that the Bible supports two opposing views such as dichotomy and trichotomy as though God didn't know how he made man. Both positions may be wrong, but it is logically untenable that the Bible teaches both views as being correct.

The teaching and practicing of discipleship, the one-to-one relationship between believers where the spiritual life is applied, is almost disappearing in some schools. The behavioral sciences have all but taken this vital ministry away from the body of Christ. Rather than discipling believers, psychotherapists are treating symptoms, many of which would never have surfaced had the people been properly grounded in the Scriptures through proper discipleship training.

Christian psychology and psychologists have been at center stage for the past generation. Since much of the material written by Christian psychologists mentions very little about the centrality of the Cross or the exchanged life, one would assume that their counseling practices also emphasize a decided humanistic bias. This doesn't mean that such psychologists do not utilize Scripture nor point people to the Lord Jesus Christ. Evangelism may be emphasized but the message of the Cross and the discipleship growth which is to follow salvation may be all but missing. The same can be said of the pastoral counselor or biblical counselor who does not teach the exchanged life as the overall direction to be given to the one being counseled.

Perhaps some would say I was not being fair or accurate to claim that many Christian counselors are working from a humanistic bias. I make the claim because both the counseling and the application of such counsel can be done in the strength of the flesh. Whether or not we want to accept it, a type of therapy has occurred any time the flesh is strengthened, whether by a pastoral counselor, biblical counselor, or a Christian psychologist or psychiatrist.

No one could successfully argue that the roots of psychology and psychiatry are not humanistic in origin. Adding Scripture without changing the core retains the inherent humanism. To accept the therapy done by a Christian which is based on any philosophy but the centrality of the Cross is humanistic.

Not only do some Christian psychologists and counselors omit the exchanged life from their methodology, some are also openly opposing those who try to keep the Cross central in scriptural counseling.

How did the church get away from discipleship and leave the vacuum for humanistic psychologists to proclaim a counterfeit gospel? And why do so many ministers who really want to help people leave the ministry to earn degrees in psychology? What are our ministerial students getting or what are they not getting which leaves them open to such a deception? Some schools do sense the need and implement their own programs. But are these counseling programs being implemented in seminaries any different from secular programs which are based on a humanistic model of man? These are questions we need to ask ourselves.

THE CHRISTIAN SCHOOL

From the fundamental Bible school to the liberal seminary there seems to be very little emphasis on any kind of counseling except that based on humanistic philosophies developed by the world system. Some of the fundamentalist schools downplay counseling as unnecessary, saying that solid biblical preaching will meet all the needs of the people. Such a belief has prevented theologically sound Bible colleges from developing any kind of comprehensive counseling program. The members of such churches are regularly turning elsewhere

114

to find answers to problems with which their pastors are either untrained or unwilling to deal.

Bible colleges that teach psychology use secular textbooks almost exclusively, since there are so few psychology texts written from a Christian viewpoint. Many educators consider psychology as just another science which has only to do with the soul or personality. They see no conflict in a separate treatment regimen for soul troubles. They conclude that the physical body has the medical profession to meet its needs and the church and the theologian to meet man's spiritual needs. Then why not the psychologist to meet man's soul needs? Such an argument cannot stand, because man is not three, but one person, interrelated and incapable of division without incurring death. Nearly nineteen centuries before the advent of psychology Jesus was promising abundant life and the Apostle Paul was telling believers of newness of life available through the Cross. It is hard to believe that this abundant life did not include the possibility of a healthy personality as well, that it dealt only with problems of the spirit and not of the soul.

In concert with the use of secular texts, most Christian colleges would subscribe to, if not inculcate, some approach to psychotherapy as a treatment regimen. Indeed, the Christian who practices psychotherapy is highly regarded in Christian circles, though few inside or outside the discipline discern the net result of psychotherapy from a spiritual vantage point. In the final analysis, therapy without the exchanged life results in the strengthening of the flesh as the mental and emotional symptoms improve.

It is not unusual for a Christian college to admit that the emphasis in its counseling or psychology major is not inherently Christian. Such statements should cause at least some raised eyebrows at the very least, but they are often accepted without comment.

115

Some seminaries, in recent years, have established majors and graduate degrees in counseling. Usually they teach their ministerial students to refer extremely troubled people to professionals in the behavioral sciences. Often the counseling approach taught by the seminary and the counselor to whom troubled people are referred are heavily influenced by one or more theorists of the humanistic tradition. Despite a scriptural veneer that some place on their theories, the core remains basically humanistic.

A common failing of Christian counseling programs is that a complete integration of the theological position of the school and the counseling model (man and methods) is never made. With some seminaries this integration is all but impossible since they don't take a single theological position on such issues as the immaterial makeup of man. Evidently it seems more intellectually palatable or politically expedient to avoid taking a stand which might cause friction or interdisciplinary competition.

The model of man used by the counseling department of such an institution might bear no resemblance to the view held by the theology department. Some students in a seminary counseling major were told that what they learned in theology would have little bearing on their counseling studies.

Christian counseling must be theologically sound or it is not Christian counseling. If there is no correspondence between an institution's theological message and its implementation in counseling, one might have to admit the possibility that a double message or "another gospel" is being proclaimed.

If a college or seminary fails to take a position on the nature of man, the institution may have a difficult time explaining intrapersonal functioning of man. If the counseling department followed suit and looked to humanistic philosophies or psychological models concerning the makeup of man, it would be difficult to portray and define in a functional sense such terms in Scripture as flesh, old man, new man, spirit, soul, and sin.

The world is afraid of absolutes because it has no source or benchmark upon which to base them. As Christians, we have the infallible Word of God so we are without excuse. Why, then, are we hesitant to take a stand on what we believe and insist that everything from our world view to our counseling approach must be consistent with that stance? Are we afraid we may appear uneducated, or do we simply not have a position with which we are sufficiently comfortable to anchor our lives and reputations? Unless and until a person has a counseling approach firmly anchored in the Word of God, one that he is certain is in tune with what the Spirit is doing to transform a life, he is understandably reluctant to let go of the humanistic system which may provide at least some results, even though they be transient solutions.

Another contention heavily dependent on world-system thinking is that counseling is a specialty which is not the domain of the pastor. Certainly the Holy Spirit places no premium on ignorance, but neither does he restrict himself to working only through someone who has an academic degree in the behavioral sciences. When therapy is the method and beneficial change is the goal, it behooves the practitioner to avail himself of every educational opportunity. When the Holy Spirit is the agent of transformation and the exchanged life is the goal, education can be a liability unless the counselor is fully yielded to the Scripture's authority and the Holy Spirit's control.

In spiritual counseling the first priority is to come to know a Person, not a method. It is not so much a technique to be learned as a relationship to be shared. This being true, it is the duty of every pastor called of God to lead his people into the exchanged life, the walk in the Spirit. To stop short of this is to fail to disciple the person. Jesus said, "Whosoever doth not bear his cross, and come after me, cannot be my disciple" (Luke 14:27).

As a result of the unclear direction from Bible schools and seminaries, many pastors are using counseling techniques that belie their theology and pulpit ministry without being aware of it. They deal with marital conflicts, financial irresponsibility, sexual incompatability, emotional symptoms, aberrant behavior, and the like rather than leading a person to appropriate by faith the results of union with Christ and with the goal of treating the problems from that stance. In treating only symptoms they strengthen the flesh with the net result of relieving symptoms, but not really treating the cause.

Alleviation of such symptoms is all too frequently equated with the resolution of the problem. Unless the axe is laid to the root of the problem, the self-life, trimming off the branches will merely result in a more flourishing tree. The symptoms that surface later may be different and often are worse than their predecessors. Counseling designed to make a person stronger and better able to handle his problems is basically flawed. It is only as he becomes weaker that a person is forced to rely upon Christ as his strength (2 Corinthians 12:9). When he abandons his own resources, he becomes a candidate for reckoning upon the results of his own death and resurrection with Christ. However, if some well-meaning Christian helps him marshall his remaining strength to cope or find a way out in his own strength, circumstances will have been successfully subverted and God's purposes in the adversity will have been thwarted.

The Christian or counselor who himself has not been reduced in strength to the place where the Cross has become a revealed reality will not relate to the process delineated above. Thus, he will object strenuously to such a course of action. Upon hearing my testimony of how God had dealt with my life in this manner, a renowned Christian counselor replied, "I can explain to you what happened in another way." His comment may have been true. I grant that it is possible to attempt to explain away the miracle wrought in me by the Holy Spirit as he transformed my life. The same could possibly have been said of all Christ's miracles. The unrenewed mind is always seeking natural ways to describe the supernatural.

I would seriously like to know how the miracle that the Spirit of God wrought that night in my life could be explained in any other way without man's taking credit in some form. It is now history that thousands of lives have been miraculously transformed in the same manner by the direct intervention of the Holy Spirit.

THE LOCAL CHURCH

Many pastors, following the lead of the Bible schools and seminaries, tend to conduct their ministries in a manner consistent with their training. Since ministerial students generally are not trained to counsel with those who have moderate to severe disturbances, they are told to refer people to the professionals. Thus, the minister can honestly state that such problems are beyond his training. Unfortunately, the problem may also be beyond his spiritual experience.

There is a time when referrals are absolutely necessary. When the person is not dealing with reality and has no one to see to his safety and that his basic needs are fulfilled, commitment to a psychiatric ward is presently the only viable alternative. Those who are chronic psychotics do not usually respond well to outpatient treatment or counseling. The individual who is in his first psychotic episode may respond very quickly. Blessed is the counselor who has a close working relationship

119

with a Christian psychiatrist to whom he may refer a troubled patient so that spiritual counseling can begin as soon as the client is again dealing with reality.

The pastor today can no longer be effective with his people only as a preacher from the pulpit. In a world characterized by alienation, a person must discover how his needs can be fully met in the Lord Jesus Christ, or his relationships with others become more and more distant. The proximity of pulpit and pew obviously involves distance, and some pastors operate more comfortably with the security and invulnerability provided by the remoteness of the pulpit.

The message of the gospel must never change, but the method of aiming it should be suited to those who hear it. Saved or unsaved, a person must be met where he is if the message is to be relevant to his situation.

When a person is starved for fellowship and interpersonal contact, an impersonal approach to the gospel is not likely to have a warm reception. Opportunities for one-to-one and small group interaction are important means of relating to people today.

Preaching, too, becomes more effective in a setting of transparency and vulnerability. In this vital context, the life and love of the Lord Jesus Christ become the spiritual medium of exchange through which the treasures of heaven are perceived and received.

A quick look at the churches that draw people in great numbers will reveal that they are providing ample opportunity for people to find love and acceptance. Unconditional acceptance is a welcome feeling to those who feel alienated. One has only to look at the rapid growth of the cults to see evidence of this. The cults usually lure seeking young people by displaying the warmth and acceptance for which they have been searching.

The cults capitalize on the estrangement of individuals from their families, God, and themselves, while

Christians, whose major commodity should be love, often seem prone to withdraw into their sanctuaries and refuse to get involved. There is no wonder that young and old alike are insisting that the church is no longer meeting their needs.

Getting involved is not exclusively a pastoral responsibility. But the pastor must set the pace. The decision to get involved and meet the needs of people must be backed up with the ability to provide scriptural answers. The key is discipleship, and both pastor and people must be disciples if they are to disciple others. If Christians have never entered into a life of discipleship, if Galatians 2:20 has no meaning for them, they probably won't be used of God to lead others into a life of identification with the death and resurrection of the Lord Jesus Christ.

The New Testament does not encourage discipleship as an option but makes it a mandate for the whole church. The life of the first-century church was a direct reflection of the discipleship emphasis and practice. A return to discipleship and disciple-making will do much to empty the psychologists' waiting rooms, since the local church will be equipped to do what it never should have ceased doing.

THE CHURCH, REJECTION, AND HUMANISM
Eleven

Although this chapter could easily become a book, I would not have completed this task without pointing out some of the encroachments of humanism in church theology and practice. Some of those who are exercised the most about secular humanism would do well to investigate the degree to which the Cross is omitted from their own lives and ministries.

Too many church programs and practices fail to take into consideration the centrality of the Cross. This failure makes it unlikely that the needs of rejected and rejecting people will be met. When people try in their own self-effort to apply scriptural principles, they are employing just another form of humanism. One has only to look at the expenditure of funds for churches and church-related facilities to see whether emphasis is being put on the place or the people. Throughout the history of the church expensive cathedrals have been built to house those entrapped in physical and spiritual poverty. They were asking for spiritual bread and were literally given stones, in beautiful architecture. One might question as to whether the works brought more glory to man or to God.

It is ironic that we believe firmly in the Scriptures, which teach that the church, the body of Christ, is made up of believers. Then we may seem to deny that statement by spending more money on buildings than people. It is true that buildings are for people, and that everything we do, even the buildings in which we worship, should glorify God. But the question is raised in terms of the emphasis or the motive for choosing extravagant buildings and deemphasizing the needs of the people. Many who come for counseling have said that they do not attend such ornate churches because they feel uncomfortable and rejected because of their clothing which appears shabby in contrast to the extravagant buildings and furnishings. Such expressions remind us of a command that we shouldn't be respecters of persons.

When human-effort approaches to ministry are in the ascendency in our churches, it should jar us awake when we realize that so many Christians never enter into the quality of victory God provided for us. When sinners are saved they become saints who can yet sin. But since the old man is dead in God's sight, the old identity is dead also. If their identity is based only on behavior, and if they are yet sinners, how could they ever be acceptable or accepted in God's sight? Humanistic thinking has pervaded this vital aspect of the believer's identity.

It is just such humanistic thinking (that we are able to improve ourselves) that has produced a weak, ineffective church, which turns to elaborate programs of self-help techniques developed by the world, veneered with a few Bible verses, and adapted for a Christian audience. When what the church has to offer is impotent to meet the deep-seated needs of Christians, the counseling offered by the church or recommended by the church is usually something other than the teaching of the exchanged life or the experienced Cross.

123

When this is the case, humanistic thinking has invaded the counseling room, even though the scriptural veneer may all but obscure the true nature of the approach.

The basic philosophy of secular humanism is now firmly implanted in the philosophy of public education in this country. In its varying forms, secular humanism is an influence to be reckoned with in all parts of the world. Though the ideas behind it are not new, the philosophy is as effective as if it had been codified into a secular religion of sorts. As such, it qualifies for tax support and is readily propagated through the public school system. Since no "deity" can be identified and no services are held, there is no apparent confusion of church and state roles, but its philosophical insistence that there is no God is as religious in nature as those who believe that there is a God, who ought to have influence on what is taught in the classrooms.

Dr. Paul Vitz, in *Psychology As Religion, the Cult of Self-Worship* (Grand Rapids: Eerdmans, 1977), has pointed out that psychology is the logical discipline to be most impacted by the tenets of humanism. As self is, in effect, enthroned as deity, all other gods must take second place. In this matter, religious humanism differs little from the secular variety. Self is exalted in both, though the avenues of its manifestation may differ.

It is not just the subject of humanism that we are addressing. It is, rather, the subtle influences of humanistic thinking that have an effect on our perception of biblical truth and the dissemination of that truth through our churches, missions, educational institutions, and in the counseling room.

As a person tries to live the Christian life in his own strength, however devout and dedicated he may be, a form of humanism is being portrayed. Dedicated self-effort is being promoted by a host of sectarian biases with little or no recognition of the inherent hindrance to true revival. To understand the inroads that humanistic thinking is having, one needs to assess the effects it is having on the various facets of Christian endeavor.

Evangelism. All of the approaches to evangelism which are being used of God to bring the lost to himself place proper emphasis on the blood of Jesus Christ being shed for our sins. Thus, the new believer knows how to deal with individual sins, but he is often left ignorant as to the scriptural answer to the power of sin. For such a person, dealing with the continuing sin in his life becomes a do-it-yourself Christianity, trying to live the Christian life in one's own strength with the Holy Spirit as "helper."

Most Christians put a proper emphasis on salvation by grace through faith, but afterward, most believers think they have to struggle for acceptance and maturity. In other words, it comes across to them that believers are justified solely on the basis of faith in the finished work of Christ, but that we are sanctified, or progress toward maturity, on the basis of our efforts. This is a contradiction of Galatians 3:3: "Are ye so foolish? having begun in the Spirit, are ye now made perfect by the flesh?" The humanistic message that comes through is that salvation is by grace but acceptance or sanctification is by works.

Discipleship. Although discipline is involved in discipleship, it should be the effect, not the cause. The Bible is abundantly clear that the Cross is the gateway into the life of discipleship or the Spirit-filled life.

A life of disciplined self-effort, what we try to do in our own strength, will eventually culminate in frustration and defeat. Rigid adherence to rules and principles, however good and scriptural, is doomed to failure so long as the believer does not experientially understand the meaning of the Cross.

True discipleship has as its central focus our union

125

with Christ in his death and resurrection. For believers, this is understood sometimes as positional and not actual death and resurrection. For them, working in their own strength, practical victory will always be an elusive goal. The power for victorious living is in the Cross, our co-death and co-resurrection with Christ. "For the preaching of the cross is to them that perish foolishness; but unto us which are saved it is the power of God" (1 Corinthians 1:18).

Missions. Going to the world in our own strength and methods is going out to fail. We read much today of the strategy for missions but very little of the power necessary to carrying out the strategy. The strategy itself may be only a self-effort program, perpetuated by good men and women with good intentions, but without resurrection power and Holy Spirit direction. William Carey's plan to go to India didn't fit the mold of some Christian leaders of his day. They failed to recognize that God was leading Cary. Had he been equally humanistic in his thinking, he would never have left England, and modern missions would have had to look to someone else as its pioneer.

Due to the lack of emphasis on the experienced Cross in our schools, many students are never brought face to face with their need prior to encountering the difficulties of the foreign field.

Miles Stanford in *Green Letters* (Grand Rapids: Zondervan, 1975), listed twenty-five great people of the past who found victory through an experiential understanding of their identification with Christ. Of these it was an average of fifteen years after entering their life's work that they found victory. Until that time, they were struggling after the flesh to serve God acceptably, and seeing only scanty results from their labors.

If this be true of these people, it is not hard to believe that many missionaries going to the field today like-

126

wise have had little experiential knowledge of the Cross. Since they are going out to make disciples, they are certain to be frustrated if they themselves are not disciples.

A minister once told of his missionary sister who was getting close to retirement age. Someone asked her, "Aren't you afraid of dying on the field?"

Her reply was, "No, I died before I went to the field."

One might wish that more of our new missionaries going out could say that also with full knowledge of its implications.

The God-called missionary will have God-given results. Some missionaries have strong emotional attractions for a particular field which they could possibly mistake for a call. If they are not certain that God put them there, they may not survive when the going gets rough. Hudson Taylor was called of God and went to China by faith. Yet it was more than ten years after he reached the mission field before he came to the end of his resources and experienced the exchanged life. Afterward, it was no longer Hudson Taylor working for the Lord but the Lord working through Hudson Taylor.

In the book of Acts, it is repeatedly stated that men filled with the Holy Spirit were sent out. If this were the policy today, there would be far fewer casualties among Christian workers on the field and far greater results while they were there.

Church programs. Some churches try one program after another to spur attendance and to produce growth. Most of the emphasis on growth has to do with numbers. When the numbers are swelling and people are being saved and brought into the church, there is good reason for rejoicing. But if the new believers get plugged into a program of some kind which provides activity but not discipleship training, there may not be any real productivity from a spiritual viewpoint.

Church members, and some pastors, in counseling often say that they are extremely busy but they realize how barren they are. Well-organized programs and well-orchestrated projects may give the impression that something is happening, but spiritually, there may actually be very little gain. Some church programs are built on pure salesmanship and would continue to function and get some kind of response even without the Holy Spirit.

Unless believers come to know the indwelling Christ and his life, church for them will be ". . . a form of godliness, but denying the power thereof" (2 Timothy 3:5).

Since the church is the body of Christ, church life should be Christ-life. It is true that sometimes even our efforts done in the flesh will have some results, but only because God honors his Word. Programs which are not born of the Spirit and led by the Spirit have their origin in the flesh, humanistic effort with humanistic results, and will have minimal impact unless God honors his Word in spite of the methods and motives of those who are running the programs.

Revival. In many churches in the United States annual "revivals" are scheduled. Men may schedule the meetings but true revival is a work of the Holy Spirit. Many say that revival has taken place when an unusual number of people receive Christ, but to use the term in that context is a fallacy, for where there has never been life there can be no revival of that life.

Revival is a work of God in the lives of believers. Revived believers will be the instruments God uses to bring the lost to himself. When believers are revived, it may result in the wholesale salvation of many unbelievers around them.

Many believers begin their new lives with the notion that their lives forever after should be onward and upward. Those who expect a steady positive growth and begin to experience suffering are frequently disillusioned. Many turn to other philosophies in an effort to shore up their sagging lives and to find comfort in something or someone other than the Comforter.

It seems logical that we should try harder and grow stronger in order to succeed in the spiritual life. But at the root of the pursuit may be the humanistic attitude of self-effort.

Although the kind of brokenness that comes from adversity will never be popular, it is in our brokenness and weakness that God's strength is shown. Life comes out of death, and victory comes out of defeat. The Cross is a place of brokenness and suffering, but the Cross must come before there can be a resurrection. It was true in Christ's life. It is true in ours. "For unto you it is given in the behalf of Christ, not only to believe in him, but also to suffer for his sake. Having the same conflict which ye saw in me, and now hear to be in me" (Philippians 1:29, 30). "Looking unto Jesus the author and finisher of our faith; who for the joy that was set before him endured the cross, despising the shame, and is set down at the right hand of the throne of God" (Hebrews 12:2).

Counseling. Perhaps the greatest impact of humanism has come through the philosophies or personality theories of psychiatrists and psychologists. Most of the major theorists begin with man and end with man, with no reference to the scriptural view of man as a creation of God. Some take an eclectic approach while others tend to emphasize methodology which deals more with behavior, feeling or thinking, or a combination of the two such as in so-called rational-emotive therapy.

Prior to the 1950s, evangelical pastors were reluctant to cooperate with psychologists and psychiatrists. However, the last thirty years have seen a rise in Christian psychology until it is now widely embraced by the church and church schools and colleges. Some of the Christian schools employ psychologists or psychiatrists to teach pastoral counseling courses.

Psychotherapy, by definition, seeks to help man to meet his own needs or to teach him how to cope with his day-to-day problems. God is rarely brought into the therapy session at all. If he is mentioned, it is usually more in the sense of evangelism and dealing with the person's sins than the believer's relationship to the Cross. Although a few Scripture verses may be used, the basic philosophy of self-help remains the same.

Because such well-known psychologists teach at reputable schools and speak at major conferences around the country, almost no one questions the foundations of their teachings. When such well-known teachers and reputable schools are offering unquestioned, unchallenged credence to each other, lay people, who are neither well-versed in psychology or theology, are hard pressed to offer meaningful criticism of what appears to them to be a closed system.

The Christian psychologist or counselor might make every attempt to bring his faith to bear in the counseling room. Or he may practice the therapy he learned in the university in much the same way he was taught. Some would be zealous in leading clients to Christ and encouraging church attendance, Scripture reading, and prayer. However, deep-seated emotional and mental symptoms usually do not respond to teaching about Christ's sacrifice for sins when the exchanged life is omitted, and when therapy takes precedence over the ministry of the Holy Spirit.

Unless the Cross as the means of experiencing the exchanged life is clearly presented and understood, the therapy will have the net effect of working with symptoms, and the real cause, the flesh or self-life, will escape undetected. Since most counselors and therapists are not prepared to recognize God's work in dealing with people through their brokenness as his means of bringing them to the Cross experience, it naturally would not be the major thrust of the counseling relationship.

It is true that emotional and mental symptoms may show some improvement when a person is born again and his sins are forgiven. However, the new believer has been forgiven for what he has done but not delivered from the control of the self-life until the exchanged life becomes a reality. This can and should occur simultaneously with salvation, but is not always the case except in a positional sense. Whether it be in the therapy room, the counseling office, or in the pulpit, if identification with Christ in death and resurrection is not a part of the formula, a form of do-it-yourself humanism is being promoted. Anytime a believer enters into the reality of his union with Christ, renewal or fullness or revival will take place in his life. This is not to say that a person's behavior problems will immediately clear up. A lifelong habit, bound up in the soul through the intellect, emotions, and will, may take some time to work itself to the surface. But at least the believer has the new resources of the Holy Spirit's power to work through his renewed spirit to bring about emotional health.

Believers are not really candidates for revival or identification until they come to understand that they are incapable, in their own strength, to live the Christian life. The Scriptures clearly define the flesh and the futility of the flesh trying to please God.

Recently a pastor, defeated in life and ministry, attended a Grace Fellowship conference. Halfway through a three-day conference he asked for personal counseling. During the counseling session he recognized the reason why his self-efforts approach wasn't working and surrendered totally to the Lord and claimed Christ as his life. That weekend he went home to preach at his church and came back for a five-day workshop the following week. He arrived home at 11:00 p.m. Friday and shared with his wife what he had learned at the conference. She too entered into identification with Christ. Early Saturday morning he started contacting his congregation one by one. By Monday noon he called to say he had led six church members into this new relationship with Christ, the exchanged life. Among the group were his son and daughter. Revival started in his church with many receiving Christ, and being baptized, as believers began sharing their new experience with others.

THE DEATH OF A CHURCH

All of us are familiar with churches which seem to be drying up on the vine. As the death process sets in, all kinds of transfusions, various programs, are administered, and no one wants to admit that the illness appears to be terminal. Money, personnel, contests, big names, high-class entertainment, and other well-known gimmicks may add no life to the church if the disease is truly terminal.

A dying church is like a terminally ill person. A church lives and grows physically and spiritually much like an individual believer, since the corporate life of a church is but the sum total of its individual members.

Bringing a new church into existence is like parents having a new baby. The youth and idealism associated with the new life can be both assets and liabilities. Energy is in abundance, but the lack of experience and training in parenting necessitates a lot of learning through trial and error. Those bringing a new church into existence learn many valuable lessons by trial and error also, sometimes at the expense of the baby church. With adequate nourishment, the young church grows, and begins to manifest, perhaps inadequately at first, the life of Christ.

The adolescent years are frequently stormy as the new church struggles for identity. Sibling rivalry often develops and sometimes different interest groups within the church are involved in power plays. Having to pull together to acquire property, conduct building programs, community outreach, and other corporate activities can be unifying factors. But much of the effort in establishing a new church can be accomplished by immature Christians. Construction activity and business matters use talents, experience, and, perhaps, financial resources which may require little spiritual maturity.

The excitement over the new church makes it easy to ask new friends and neighbors to come and see it and to participate in the celebration of new life. Spiritual fervor remains high and many are saved and added to the growing church. Sometimes rapid growth and lack of coordination, which can cause friction, begin to take a toll.

As the church comes of age, the old ways of doing things may no longer seem befitting a more mature church. To accomplish greater objectives, the church may decide that a new pastor is needed as they conclude that they have outgrown their old founding pastor. However, a segment of the congregation may be loyal to the pastor and decide to leave with him to start another church. The schism in the body is rationalized and justified by those who leave and those who stay. The church established by the split goes through the pangs of starting all over. Such a pattern as this unfolds itself in hundreds of churches across the land.

Meanwhile, back at the church from which the pastor came, it is necessary to form a pulpit committee to begin searching for a new pastor. Some rough guidelines are drawn up to enhance the selection procedure. Ade-

133

quate education is a must. He should be between thirty-five and forty-five years old and a family man. Frequently, more energy and politics go into the mechanics of the selection than into the vital matter of prayer, not for an able-bodied man but one who is strong in spirit, depending not on his own strength but the power of the Holy Spirit.

A flurry of activity and new programs begin, and the "transfusion" of new blood may bring a large numerical increase that may again be mistaken for real growth. When the newness of the new pastor and his programs is over and things settle into some kind of normalcy, the church may again begin to get restless. When there are buildings aplenty and sufficient personnel to make the machinery work, some members look for new frontiers to open up.

If the church during this time is not properly fed, problems like an insidious disease, may begin to eat away at the body. One symptom after another may be diagnosed as the problem, and suitable self-effort remedies may be applied. Certain teaching from the pulpit is occasionally effective, but sometimes the cure comes only when the causes, and not the symptoms, are treated.

As symptomatic treatment becomes increasingly less effective, transfusions of one sort or another may be required on a periodic basis. It may be apparent to most of the members that the church is on a treadmill, creating a lot of activity, but not getting anywhere. As programs are born, run their course, and die, new programs are frantically devised to take their place. Eventually, it seems that no amount of human effort will keep a program going for very long.

Such churches rarely die physically. Certain activity will keep them going, but it is obvious that nothing much is happening. The members, individually and corporately, are unwilling to let go of what they have, so they hang on. Very often the problem is both individual and corporate or collective. The believers understand all about salvation but few are aware of the life-in-the-Spirit principle taught in the New Testament. Each believer was baptized into the death and resurrection of the Lord Jesus Christ at the time of the new birth. Yet many of them have not gone through the process of coming to the end of themselves and their resources and begun to live in the resources of Christ.

In the same way, a church, as a corporate body of believers, must come to the end of its fleshly resources to manifest corporately the life of the Lord Jesus Christ. What happens to one individual must be the experience of each individual member of the local body if the church is to function properly.

It is only after the individuals of the church experience life out of death that it is possible to appreciate and abide in the relationship of the vine and the branch as taught in John 15, a relationship necessary for a church to function as God intended. The branch doesn't produce by a flurry of activity but by abiding where it has been placed, in the vine. Similarly, the individual believer and the church will only produce fruit as abiding in the vine becomes an experiential reality.

It is painful for an individual to come to the end of himself, but it is necessary if the life of Christ is to be made manifest in him.

When the individual lives that make up the church have gone through death into life, the composite life of the church will be the life of Christ. As members of Christ's body, we must work and pray to the end that such an example of life in Christ will be the rule and not the exception. And until believers have entered into such an understanding of this relationship in Christ, knowing as a child of God that acceptance and identity come from our relationship to Christ apart from works, the churches of which they are a part have no message to defeated believers struggling for acceptance and identity. Humanistic self-effort is not the answer. Only Christ and his Cross is.

GOD'S ANSWER TO A REJECTING SOCIETY
Twelve

When the rejection syndrome infects the lives of church people, and the effects are felt in the corporate life of the church, it should come as no surprise to learn that the effects of rejection are felt throughout society at large. The informal caste systems which we all daily experience, such as the pecking order which we find everywhere, results in both overt and covert rejection.

Those who have no relationship with the Lord Jesus Christ have no support system to heal the hurts which a rejecting society has dealt them. These hurts and rejections are passed on to others through frustration, hostility, and antisocial behavior, sometimes including violent crime.

When those in government sense that there are needs to be met and wrongs to be righted, a number of agencies step in, as a benevolent deity, to meet the needs and to judge the offenders. When these needs are attempted to be met by government, measures that the person is able to take and should be taking for himself, the government is really overprotecting its citizens in the same way that an overprotecting parent is treating his child. By overprotecting, government can also pass on rejection to its citizens by allowing them to lose their personhood. When the rejection syndrome is set in motion, self-respect is destroyed, and dependency upon the government is created. The person in such an overprotected situation becomes not a productive asset to society but a permanent liability. Such activities provide the makings of a welfare state and a welfare class.

Once people have become dependent upon government subsidies, they begin to demand even more benefits, a kind of greed which propels them down the road to destruction. Rather than teaching them to be responsible people, with a desire to develop the ability to earn their own way, and be contributing members of society, the help they are getting makes work unnecessary for them. Biblical truths are overlooked in the process. The Apostle Paul wrote: "If any would not work, neither should he eat" (2 Thessalonians 3:10). We should remember that Paul did not say, "If any *could* not work," but "*would* not work."

The benevolent deity of secular humanism is usually at odds with God's revealed truth. For example, when someone dares to oppose abortions as a violation of God's command, secular humanists call antiabortion laws an abridgment of human freedom, as if God has nothing to say about human life.

Abortion is but one of the more blatant examples of a decadent society which has rejected God and is reaping the results of its rebellion in the rapid slide toward self-destruction. Divorce statistics are another clear testimony to the giving and receiving of rejection going on in homes all across the country. Each person brings the seeds of rejection into the marriage and soon the seeds develop and do their destructive work. For every two marriages contracted each year, at least one divorce takes place. The children of these broken homes are caught in the crossfire of rejection between the parents and suffer rejection by the parents as well as suffering the trauma of separation from at least one parent.

Runaway sexual immorality, pornography, deviant behavior, occultism, obsession with violence, and crime are all indicators that society as a whole is saying, "We will not have God to rule over us." The philosophy of humanism suggests that education can be the means of paving the way to a utopian society. Yet as the numbers of those educated rise, the rate of crime increases even more.

Just as there is rejection within families and within society, so there is rejection between societies and nations, culminating in hostility and open conflict. Nations spend astronomical amounts of money to defend themselves against aggression, depleting their resources that could have gone to meet the needs of their people.

Selfishness, unbridled passion, and rebellion against God can only be conquered by a mighty movement of the Holy Spirit in our land. The day is gone when we can afford the luxury of carnal Christianity. Converting the lost to a low level of spiritual mediocrity will change their eternal destinies but it will have little effect on their present life-style.

We must begin in the church if the lost are to see a life-style which will change their lives and challenge them to commitment. When Christians are living like the world, having the same problems, and seeking the world's answers for them, the world sees no reason to become a part of our religion game. When Christians are miserable and cracking up emotionally, the lost have every right to say, "I have enough misery already. Why should I become a Christian?"

When Christians stop going to the world for answers, the world may begin to go to the church. Why should the world respect the church when we are telling them by our behavior that our answer in Christ doesn't even work for us?

We must see Christ in the lives of believers instead of the carnal, self-centered lives that typify Christianity if we are to have an impact on the world.

As such believers experience and share the message of "...Christ in you, the hope of glory" (Colossians 1:27), revival spreads from person to person and such renewal, which accepts the message of acceptance in Christ, can dispel the existing epidemic of the rejection syndrome.

May God convict each of us of the sinfulness of carnal, self-centered living in order that we might stop rejecting the Lordship of Christ. Only as Christ is Lord will we be able to manifest his life in us (2 Corinthians 4:11). When Jesus is lifted up in our lives and he lives and loves through us, people will be drawn into a right relationship with him.

Acceptance in Christ is the antidote to rejection. Those who experience rejection at the hands of others will learn it as a way of life and continue to be part of the problem. Those who find acceptance in Christ will manifest the kind of joy that will offer hope to a loveless, rejection-filled world.

There is a drought of accepting love, even in the body of Christ. It would bring change to our world if everyone could look at our churches and say, "Behold, how they love one another!" Only as we rightly relate ourselves to the Cross and begin to say, as the Holy Spirit urges us, "... not I but Christ" (Galatians 2:20), can we live his life and love others with his love.

Isaiah, in speaking of the coming Messiah, wrote: "He was despised and rejected" (Isaiah 53:3). But he endured it so that we need never know God's rejection. Paul wrote many years later: "The love of God is shed abroad in our hearts by the Holy Ghost which is given to us" (Romans 5:5). And with that God-given love, we may break the old sinful habits of rejecting others, and love them with the same unconditional love by which God accepts us and draws us to him as his children. Because of God's unconditional love, rejection ended at the Cross.